Peter Stade... ✎ YO-AVA-790

Adventure
Aquarium

Creating and Observing

With Color Photographs
by Noted Aquarium

Contents

Previous page: The splendidly colored Jewel Tetra clearly feels comfortable in a school.

A Ram pair guards and cares for its young.

The brilliant shimmering colors of the fish, their fascinating behavior, and the opportunity to make exciting observations—these are all good reasons for getting an aquarium. In this manual you will find all the advice necessary for setting up your first aquarium and taking care of it so that it will give you long-term pleasure, and so that the plants and fish will be healthy and happy.

Aquarium expert Peter Stadelmann explains in easy-to-understand terms what equipment you need and introduces some popular and easy-to-care-for fish. He names the species that get along well with each other and the plants that are most appropriate for your aquarium. You will also learn what to feed your fish and what you can do if they get sick. In addition, there are tips for observation, projects, and experiments. A list of useful terms explains important technical terms. HOW-TO pages show you step-by-step how to set up your aquarium and care for it, how to buy your fish, and how to feed your fish so that they stay healthy.

Beautiful photographs by noted aquarium photographers give a fascinating insight into the water world. The illustrations by Peter Fischer show details of aquarium technology as well as the appearance and behavior of various kinds of fish. The author and the editors of Barron's hope that you have much fun with your first aquarium.

Please read the Important Note to Parents on page 63.

Equipment for the Aquarium

An aquarium is a colorful little world of its own: a picture window that gives you a view into a part of a stream or lake in nature. Since plants and animals live in the aquarium, they need your care and help. As a proper aquarist, which of course you intend to become when you get an aquarium, you are responsible for making sure that the fish thrive in their surroundings and do not become sick.

The basic equipment: You can hardly wait to pick out your fish. But first you need some basic equipment in order to provide the fish with a "cozy home." You should only purchase the fish after your aquarium is already completely equipped. You can find all the equipment at the pet or aquarium store. The dealer can give you expert advice and take into account any special wishes you might have. He may also have a few tips for you that will make your start as an aquarist easier.

The Fire-mouth Cichlid keeps careful watch while its young swim around it.

The Right Tank

For a beginner's aquarium, I recommend a rectangular tank made entirely of glass. A good size to start with is 24 in (60 cm) long, 12 in (30 cm) wide, and 16 in (41 cm) high. This holds 20 gallons (75 L) of water. All my suggestions for arrangement and decorations, for plants and fish, are based on a tank with these dimensions. You can thus be sure that everything you find here in this book will be exactly right for your tank.

Lighting

Light for fish and plants: You have to illuminate your aquarium artificially, because the daylight that comes into your room isn't enough. The artificial light replaces the sun outside. Since most aquarium fish come from tropical areas where it stays daylight for 12 to 14 hours all year long without varying, you also need at least 12 hours of "sunlight" per day in your aquarium for the fish to feel comfortable. In addition, plants need light to assimilate (make food, see Useful Terms, page 58).

Lighting in the cover: I recommend that you illuminate the aquarium by means of a full-sized cover. It is simply set on top of the aquarium and contains a fluorescent bulb. I advise using a bulb that produces a warm, slightly yellowish light; this color makes the plants on short stems grow bushy and gives them a deep green color. I advise against a fluorescent bulb with a cold, violet light. It does indeed make the fish look more colorful, but it exaggerates the colors, making the green of the plants appear pale. Besides, the violet light makes the plants grow longer stems and smaller leaves.

Duration: It is important for fish and plants that the light shine over the aquarium for the same length of time every day. A lighting duration of 12 to 14 hours per day corresponds to the length of the day in the tropics. This makes the fish feel the best and ensures that the plants have enough light to assimilate. To keep you from forgetting to turn on the light at the proper time, you can regulate it with a timer. Then every morning the light goes on auto-

The male Fighting Fish painstakingly spits each egg into the bubble nest.

matically and off again every evening—whether you are home or not.

Heating

All the fish that I recommend in this book require warm water (with the exception of Goldfish; see page 26). Therefore you must heat the water in the aquarium or your fish will get sick. It's best if you use a 50-watt electric heater for this. It warms the water to the desired temperature, and also keeps it constant.

The thermostatic heater: A heater with a built-in thermostat is very practical, because it allows the water temperature to be maintained easily, for example at 77°F (25°C). If the water temperature ever drops 4° or 5°F (2° or 3°C), perhaps because you didn't have the heat on in your room in cool weather, the thermostat turns on the heating apparatus in the aquarium. When the desired temperature is reached, the thermostat automatically turns off the heat.

Important: The 50-watt thermostatic heater can only maintain the temperature; it can't heat water to 77°F (25°C). Therefore always use lukewarm water when changing water (see page 46). If your room isn't heated every day during the cold season, I recommend a more efficient heater with higher wattage. It's best to get advice from the pet or aquarium store dealer.

Thermometer: To allow you to check any time to see if the water in the aquarium is the right temperature, you need an aquarium thermometer (see Installing Equipment, page 15).

Filter

Your aquarium needs a filter to keep the water clear and clean and the fish healthy. The filter draws in the water and filters out debris such as excre-ment or the rotting remains of food.

Filter types: There are internal and external filters; both will keep your aquarium nice and clean. For your small tank I recommend that you get an interior filter, which is driven by a circulation pump. It's easier to service and very practical. You only need to fasten it in a corner of the aquarium, insert the tube—and it's up and running.

An external filter is fastened to the outside of the aquarium and is particularly suitable for large aquariums.

Function of the filter: The filter has several tasks in the aquarium. It works in two steps.

Step 1. Mechanical filtering

The circulation pump built into the filter draws in the water containing debris, such as fish excrement, food remains, or rotting plant parts, through a fine-pored filter (see Filter Mediums, page 7). There the debris is trapped in a sieve and removed at each cleaning of the filter (see Filter Care, page 44).

Step 2. Biological filtering

Tiny bacteria live in the filter medium. They break the waste deposits down into smaller parts, which are used by the plants as nutrients (see Plant Care, page 47). The mulm is what is left and is washed out of the filter medium during cleaning of the filter. (See Siphoning Off the Mulm, page 46.)

Filter Media

The filter medium, which is embedded in the filter, can consist of different materials:

Foam filter: I recommend that you get large-pored plastic foam from the pet or aquarium store to use as the filtering medium for your interior filter. It lasts for a long time and is easy to care for. If it ever becomes soft and loses its shape, you can replace it with a new one (see Filter Care, page 44).

Carbon filter: The carbon filter, which is made of a special charcoal, filters out material that is dissolved in the aquarium water. If your fish are sick and you need to give them medicine, the carbon can filter out the medicine when your fish are healthy again. The effect of the carbon filter lasts only a few days. After that it works as a mechanical filter again. Since no bacteria can colonize in it, it does not filter the aquarium water biologically. In addition, carbon filters don't have any pores and therefore have the great disadvantage that they clog up very quickly. Because they also remove useful materials like plant fertilizer from the water, you must only use carbon filters when you need to clear the remains of medications from the water.

Carbon Dioxide Fertilizers

Since there is usually not enough carbon dioxide (CO_2) available in the aquarium, you can provide your plants with additional carbon dioxide with CO_2-fertilizing equipment. The plants then grow better and can produce more oxygen (see What Are Plants Good For?, page 41). I suggest a CO_2 diffuser. This device is easy to take care of and is inexpensive. You fill the diffuser from a bottle and thus offer your plants a supply of carbon dioxide, from which they take as much out of the water as they need. You can't make any mistakes and also don't ever have to worry that there is going to be too much carbon dioxide in your aquarium.

Air Pumps

An air pump is very useful, since you can power your various pieces of equipment with it, for example, a mulm vacuum (see page 46) or an airstone. If you ever want to raise young fish (called "fry"), you need the pump for your breeding tank (see Birth Among Guppies, page 52).

Airstone: You can use this to increase the oxygen concentration in your aquarium. The airstone is made of a porous material. It is connected to the pump with a hose and expels the air into the water in many small bubbles (see drawing, page 54). However, you can only use the airstone for short periods of time. Oxygen bubbles injure the plants, because they drive the carbon dioxide that plants need to grow out of the water (see What Do Plants Need?, page 42).

Foam filter for the air pump: You need this most if you ever want to raise young fish. A small foam filter (see drawing, page 54) is, like an airstone, linked to the air pump. Its effectiveness as a filter is very good, although it creates only a small current. Also this arrangement prevents very small fry from being drawn into the filter.

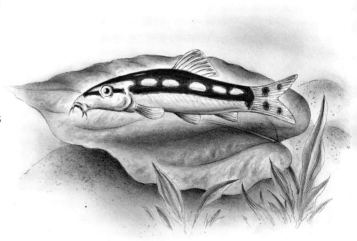

Dwarf Loaches like to hover over large leaves.

Air Valves

If you are only attaching the foam filter to the oxygen pump, you only need a single valve. You use it to adjust the air intake so that the bubbles don't go "blub-blub." The more the filter "blubs," the worse it filters.

If you want to drive more equipment at the same time, for instance a foam filter and an airstone, you need an additional valve for each additional piece of equipment. You can open and close each valve, that is every "tap connection," individually. It's like water faucets, when there are separate faucets for hot and cold water.

In the drawing of the rearing tank (see page 54) you see how the connections with the different valves look. One valve controls the airstone, the other valve controls the foam filter.

Bottom Materials and Decoration

Your aquarium needs material on the bottom in which the plants can root and obtain nutrients. You can also lay decorative objects on top of the bottom material, such as stones and driftwood.

Foundation

The foundation consists of two layers of pebbles with an interlayer of nutrient soil (see page 14).

Quartz gravel is the ideal bottom material. Gravel in sizes of 3 to 5 mm is most suitable. Coarser gravel isn't so good, because it holds too much dirt and is very hard to keep clean. Quartz gravel is also not brightly colored, which makes fish feel more comfortable than brightly colored gravel. But don't use black gravel. It absorbs too much light, which is necessary for your plants.

Sand is only suitable for fish species that like to eat on the bottom and poke around in the sand, for example, the armored catfishes and barbs. If you want to keep these species, you can provide them with a little sandy area in the aquarium. A sandy foundation is also good in a rearing aquarium because it can be simply siphoned out. Otherwise it isn't really appropriate for your aquarium. Because it compacts very easily, rotting occurs very easily in it. Besides, the plants don't grow well in sand, since it doesn't have enough oxygen available for their roots.

The nutrient layer is enriched with nitrogen fertilizer and other minerals. It provides the aquarium plants with the substances they must have to grow. When setting up your aquarium, spread the nutrient layer as a slow-release fertilizer over the bottom layer of gravel (see page 14).

Decoration

Fish need places where they can hide. Some fish (for example, cichlids) also establish territories that they defend against other members of the species. Therefore you need to decorate your aquarium with stones and driftwood.

Stones: With several stones you can build a cave that offers a haven for the fish. Only lime-free stones such as quartz, granite, lava, and red, green, and black slate are suitable. Since you can't see whether stones you've gathered yourself contain limestone, you are better off to buy stones from the pet or aquarium store.

Driftwood: Driftwood also offers good hiding places and it looks decorative. You can use driftwood that you get in the pet store without any worry. Wood that you've found outdoors must not be used in the aquarium, since it may quickly rot and foul the water.

Ceramic and clay caves: Some plants like to grow on these objects. They also

You should always take your time feeding your fish and observe them carefully as you do it.

provide the best hiding places and breeding caves for fish.

Toys: Brilliantly colored plastic plants, little fortresses, castles, sunken ships with divers, and similar aquarium toys don't disturb the fish at all. You can definitely use them as decoration material. But consider that "dead" materials are easily covered with algae (see Combatting Algae, page 45). Plastic plants cannot replace real plants in their function as oxygen producers. Therefore you absolutely must have living plants in

your aquarium, too. Without them the aquarium cannot function (see What Are Plants Good For?, page 41).

Other Equipment

Fish nets are useful for removing fish or loose leaves. You need a fine-meshed net for fry and a coarser-meshed net for the adult fish.

An algae cleaner serves for cleaning the aquarium glass (see page 47). You can buy it as a magnetic cleaner or as a razor blade cleaner.

A *mulm vaccuum* is good to have for cleaning the bottom (see page 46). It is driven by an air pump and functions like a vaccuum cleaner. It simply sucks up the dirt particles from the gravel.

Plastic bucket, hose, and watering can are needed for changing the water. To keep the bucket and watering can from being used for anything else, you should label them.

What Doesn't Belong in the Aquarium

You shouldn't put into the aquarium any plants you find outside, limestone, sea mussels, fresh coconut shells, or painted toys, whose color may dissolve in the water. These objects change the water quality and could poison your fish. Also, sharp-cornered or pointed objects have no place in an aquarium, since the fish can be injured on them. If necessary, ask your pet store dealer what you can put in the aquarium.

The Back Wall of the Aquarium

To make sure that you'll see the colorful fish in your aquarium rather than the pattern of your wallpaper, you need a background for the aquarium, in front of which the fish and the plants will show up well. I advise a photographed back wall from the pet store. You can also paint an underwater landscape yourself. Tape the photographed back wall or your own picture to the outside back of the aquarium.

Buying Plants

You can buy the plants one to two days before you set up your aquarium. But don't just pick out anything; rather, follow my planting suggestions (see page 15). This guarantees that the plants and fish will fit well in your aquarium and with each other.

Tips for Buying

• - Take your time and get advice from the pet or aquarium store dealer.
• Get explanations of how the technical apparatus function, and ask to be shown how you attach them to the aquarium.
  • Keep all the warranties for the equipment in a safe place with the sales receipts. At home, open the original packing carefully and keep it for four weeks. This is important if you have to return something. Usually there is an exchange only when original packaging, sales slip, and warranties are presented.

Safety Around the Aquarium

Water and electricity can lead to dangerous accidents. Therefore you should make absolutely sure when buying equipment that it is also really suitable for use in an aquarium.

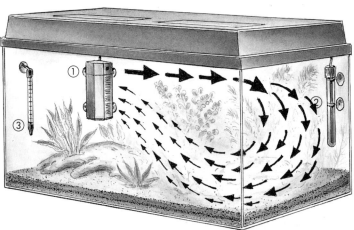

An aquarium set up and ready for fish:
① Foam internal filter, ② rod heater, ③ thermometer. The arrows show the water circulation.

• Every technical device must have the UL sticker on it (see Useful Terms, page 58). These letters give the assurance that the safety of the equipment has been carefully checked by experts and that "with ordinary use" (as the experts say) nothing dangerous can happen.

• Always unplug any electrical equipment before you do any cleaning around or in the aquarium.
• Never do your own repairs on the aquarium or the equipment if there is something wrong with it. As a matter of principle, all repairs should only be carried out by an expert.

Shopping List for Your 24-in (60-cm) Aquarium

This is a list of everything you need as basic equipment.

1 all-glass aquarium (24 × 12 × 16 in. [60 × 30 × 41 cm]), with or without decorative molding
1 Styrofoam sheet, ½ in. (10 mm) thick (only for an aquarium without decorative moldings)
6 bags of quartz gravel at 5½ lb. (2.5 kg) each (gravel size 3 to 5 mm, not too light)
1 package of nutrient soil for 20 gal (75 L)
3 roundish lime-free stones
1 flattish lime-free stone
1 aquarium root
1 can of water conditioner

1 circulating pump interior filter with foam filter cartridge
1 thermostatic heater (50 watt) with temperature markings
1 aquarium cover with built-in fluorescent tube (15 watts; color 41)
1 aquarium thermometer
1 background
1 lighting timer
1 grounded plug
1 bucket (10 qt [10 L])
1 hose for water changing (59 in [1.5 m] long, 12- to 16-mm diameter)
1 watering can
1 algae cleaner (magnet or blade)
plants (see Planting Suggestions, page 15)

Setting Up the Aquarium

Finally you're ready. You have purchased the aquarium, the technical equipment, and the water plants. Now you can start arranging your little water world. But even if you'd prefer to plunge right in, you'd be better off to wait until the next weekend, when you have enough time to set up the aquarium in peace and quiet. Nothing is more annoying than having to begin all over again just because you made a mistake in a hurry.

Some Chores First

Before you can really get started, there are some things you have to do first. It's best if you take care of them a day ahead; then you can finally tackle the arrangement of the aquarium the next day. You should lay out the following items for your preparations: two plastic basins, a bucket, and a brush.

Preparing the plants: Put the aquarium plants that you bought one or two days ago in a basin of water (keep it dark and cool) until you are ready to plant them. This way they will keep fresh. Pick out wilted plants and throw them away; they won't recover.

Testing the tank: Check carefully to be sure that the tank has survived the trip home. If you don't find any cracks on the first look, do a general test with water. Carefully place the tank in the bathtub on the Styrofoam pad and fill it with water. After a short time check to see whether it is watertight. If the water runs out, take it back, with the

A Cichlid caring for the fry. He fans his fins to produce oxygen and watches to see that no other fish come too near.

sales slip, to the dealer from whom you bought it. He or she will certainly replace it.

Preparing the bottom and decorative materials:
• New clay and ceramic containers can be used after rinsing with clear water. They have no effect on the water. Don't use already-used flower pots or similar materials. They may contain various poisonous substances—such as flower fertilizer, for instance—that could get into the aquarium water.
• Clean the wood thoroughly with the brush under running water. Then leave it overnight in a bucket of warm water. It will then absorb the water and later stay on the bottom of the aquarium. If the wood floats on the surface in the bucket of water, weight it down with a flat stone.
• Scrub all stones that you want to place in the aquarium very thoroughly with the brush.

Clear water is good enough for this purpose. You shouldn't use any soap or cleaners, because any residue in your aquarium water could be poisonous.
• You must also thoroughly wash the gravel for the floor of the aquarium. To do this, you put the gravel in a large basin, then hold it at an angle under running water. At the same time stir the pebbles with your hand until the flowing water runs clear. Be extra careful not to let any pebbles go down the drain. It gets stopped up very easily and is then very difficult to clear again.

Leopard Catfish prefer to stay in the bottom regions.

Dry Run

While the aquarium is still empty, you can comfortably play with the decoration materials and try sample arrangements. This way you can see if you like your arrangement before adding water to the tank.

Note: When decorating, the principle to follow is "less is more." The fish need room to swim, and some plants need room to grow. Therefore you shouldn't cover the entire floor of the aquarium with decorative material.

Getting the Aquarium Running

When your aquarium is arranged (see HOW-TO: Setting Up, pages 14 and 15), you can get it running. Put the cover with the fluorescent bulb on the aquarium, plug it into the wall, set the timer to a lighting schedule of 12 to 14 hours, and turn on the light. There it is: your own first aquarium. And it looks terrific, even if there are no fish swimming in it yet.

HOW-TO:
Setting Up

Arranging the aquarium is simple, and you can certainly do it without any difficulty if you just do it the way it is explained here. You will find the necessary materials on the shopping list (see page 11).

Setting Up the Tank

Setting up: Place the empty tank where you want to keep your aquarium. If it has no decorative moldings, it must stand on a ½-in.- (1-cm-) thick Styrofoam pad. This smooths out any unevenness in the surface underneath that might stress the glass and break it. An aquarium with decorative moldings can stand directly on a shelf or table. Consider that when your aquarium is full it weighs about 132 lb. (60 kg). The stand, shelf, or table must be able to bear this weight. You can get an appropri-

1. Smooth out the individual layers with your fingers.

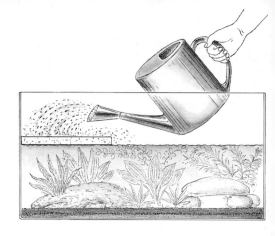

2. So as not to stir up the bottom, direct the stream from the watering can at a piece of Styrofoam.

ately stable stand or cabinet in the pet or aquarium store.

Cleaning: Wipe down the tank thoroughly with a cloth and clear, warm water.

Putting in the Bottom Materials
Drawing 1

1. *Gravel:* Distribute three bags of washed gravel on the floor of the tank and smooth it out with your fingers.

2. *Fertilizer:* Distribute the fertilizer layer for the plants smoothly on top of the gravel.

3. *Gravel:* Distribute the remaining three bags of washed gravel on top and smooth it out. Let the bottom surface slope up a little toward the back, since the plants with deeper roots will be placed here.

Decorating the Tank

You can give free rein to your imagination here. Anything is permitted, so long as it doesn't injure the fish or poison the water (see What Doesn't Belong in the Aquarium, page 10).

Stone caves: You can build a cave with four stones. Arrange

three stones in a triangle, lay a big, flat stone over them, and the hideaway is complete.

Wood: You can lay the wood on the gravel opposite the stone cave. It also provides places for the fish to hide. You can also fasten a plant to it (see Distributing the Plants in the Tank, below).

Putting in the Water
Drawing 2

Now put a piece of Styrofoam or a plastic plate (measuring 8 × 12 in. [20 × 30 cm]) in a corner of the tank and fill the tank one-third full with lukewarm tap water. To do this, use a watering can that is used only for this purpose to pour the water onto the Styrofoam so as not to stir up the bottom. Then take the Styrofoam out again.

Distributing the Plants in the Tank
Drawing 3

Below I recommend some plants that are particularly easy to care for. Since they grow to different heights, I'll also tell you where it's best to put them. The shortest plants go in the foreground, the medium ones in the middle, and the tallest ones in the background. Drawing 3 shows you how your aquarium will look with plants.

Foreground: Dwarf Amazon Sword (*Echinodorus grisebachii*) covers the bottom.

Middleground: The Red Amazon Sword plant (*Echinodorus osiris*) goes in between the stone cave and the driftwood; Java Fern (*Microsorium pteropus*) is fastened to the wood with nylon thread; Walker's Water Trumpet (*Cryptocoryne walkeri*) goes behind the piece of wood; Floating Fern (*Ceratopteris cornuta*) floats on the water's surface.

Background: Argentinian Waterweed (*Egeria densa*) and Water Hyssop (*Bacopa caroliniana*) are placed close to the back wall.

Putting in the Plants
Drawing 4

Rosette plants often come planted in little pots with rock wool.

• Turn over the little pot, strike it gently against the edge of a table, and pull out the plant.

Carefully free it from the rock wool.

• With a pair of scissors, shorten the roots to a maximum of one-third of their total length. Never pinch off the roots with your fingers since you can crush them that way, which causes them to rot.

• Scratch a little hollow in the gravel with your fingers, set the plant in it, and then close the planting hole again (see drawing 4).

• Now gently pull the plant upward slightly. This way you avoid bending the roots.

Stem plants should be laid flat on the gravel and weighted with a pebble (see drawing 4, page 47). Anchored this way, the plant puts out roots in several places at once and grows quickly.

Putting in the Rest of the Water
When the tank is arranged and planted, it is filled with water up to 2 in. (5 cm) from the top edge. You need to leave that much space free to keep the

water from overflowing when you add the technical equipment. You need to be somewhat careful when you add the water so as not to wash the plants out of their locations. So aim the stream of water at the piece of Styrofoam, as you have done already, and then remove the Styrofoam from the aquarium when you are finished.

4. The rosette plant is held in the hole. Then the pebbles are piled in around the plant.

Installing the Equipment
• Attach the filter and the heater to the back of the tank in each corner, with their suction cups against the glass.

• The thermometer goes to the left on the front surface of the aquarium glass. Thus you can read the water temperature anytime (see drawing, page 10).

• Now fill the tank with water up to about ½ in. (1 cm) from the top edge.

• Finally, add the iron fertilizer for the plants (see Taking Care of the Plants, page 47). Now you're finished: you can start up your aquarium (see page 13).

3. Planting suggestions.
1: Dwarf Amazon Sword,
2: Red Amazon Swords,
3: Java Fern,
4: Walker's Water Trumpet
5: Floating Fern,
6: Waterweed, and
7: Water Hyssop.

15

An Aquarium Without Fish Is Boring!

You're right, but for the sake of the fish you must still have a little patience until the aquarium is conditioned (see Watching and Wondering, right). What does that mean? It takes time for the tap water with which you've filled the tank to turn into suitable aquarium water. The plants need time to root firmly. The filter bacteria, which contribute to clean water, must colonize the filter medium. Only after these things happen has a healthy living space developed from what is now still an uncomfortable environment for the fish.

When can the fish finally be added? I recommend that you not buy the fish until the aquarium has been well conditioned. You will know when it's ready because the water, which was very cloudy at first, will become clear again. You shouldn't buy the fish before that because you have to keep them in plastic bags, and then they aren't happy at all. The bags are only good for transporting them from one place to another.

The Platy is an easy fish to care for.

Watching and Wondering Conditioning the Aquarium

Even without fish, in the next few days there is much to wonder at in the aquarium. The water can be cloudy or even brownish and full of air bubbles. In the first few days your aquarium might be cloudy at night and the next morning as clear as glass. White slime can coat the glass. This is all completely normal and shows how the water gradually is changing to good aquarium water in which the fish will feel completely comfortable."

True aquarists say: "The aquarium is becoming conditioned

Cloudy water results from fertilizer that is stirred up from the bottom and dissolved in the water. Plants and the filter contribute to making the cloudiness slowly disappear. The plants take up the fertilizer as "food" little by little, and the filter removes the larger particles from the water. Eventually the water clears.

Brownish water is frequently caused by the aquarium wood, which gives off tannic or humic acid (see Useful Terms, page 58). The color of the water is not harmful and later disappears almost completely with regular changes of water (see page 46).

White slime on the glass forms with the colonization of bacteria, which feed on the protein that is present in the water. However, the slime is completely harmless both to the plants and the fish. It is later either eaten by the snails in your aquarium or removed when you clean the glass (see page 47). Preliminary cleaning of the glass is unnecessary.

Fish as a Present?

Tell all your friends and relatives not to give you any fish. Otherwise you will

Visiting the Purple Cichlid family. The mother watches over her young from the cave.

receive fish from different aquariums and thus from different water qualities. It could easily be that a fish introduces a disease that you may have difficulty curing. Also, fish should get along well with each other (see Selecting the Fish Species, page 18). Nevertheless if your friends surprise you with a bag of fish, you had best follow the emergency program below.

Emergency Program

Suppose the aquarium isn't properly conditioned, but you have already put fish in it, perhaps because you received some as a present. You notice that they aren't feeling well, that their color is pale, and they clamp their fins fearfully. The only help left is to undertake the following program:

1. Change a third of the water every three days (see page 46) and add the water preparation chemicals according to the directions on the package.

2. Feed the fish only moderately and with flakes, not frozen food. Also put vitamins in the aquarium water (see Proper Feeding, page 33).

3. Don't fertilize plants now but only when the aquarium is conditioned.

You must follow this program conscientiously for about two weeks. Then you will have "soothed" the aquarium and you can go back to the normal patterns of care (see HOW-TO: Proper Care, pages 46 and 47).

You must wait another two weeks before you may add more fish.

HOW-TO:
Buying the Fish

When your aquarium is conditioned, you can go pick out your fish at the pet or aquarium store. There you will have the task of choosing, for you have to make a selection, and that isn't so easy.

Selecting the Fish Species

Since not all species of fish get along with each other, you have to be careful in making your selection. You shouldn't buy fish according to their colors alone.

• The behavior patterns of the fish species must harmonize with one another. There are playful fish, which pull on the long fins of other fish and thereby annoy them; and there are bullies, which make life difficult for the more peaceful species.

• For your small tank, the only species appropriate are fish that don't grow too large. It would be best for you to follow my suggestions (see page 31). If you want to know more, the pet or aquarium store dealer will be glad to help you.

• The fishes' requirements for water temperature and quality must match (see Easy-Care Fish, page 26).

• Every fish species has a preferred living area (see the Body Shape of the Fish, page 20). Some like to hover near the surface of the water, others in the middle region, and still others near the bottom. To make the best use of the aquarium and to offer each species the largest possible territory, I recommend that you put one species in each area.

The proper fish community: All the fish in my Suggested Combinations (see page 31) get along well with each other. If you would rather make a combination of your own selections, you should find out about their exact requirements before you buy them. The pet or aquarium store dealer will also give you advice on how to choose the fish.

Tips for Buying Fish

Be sure that you bring home healthy fish.

• Only buy fish from well-cared-for aquariums (clear water, clean glass, no dead fish in the tank).

• Shop when the store isn't overrun with customers. The salesperson then has more time to advise you.

• Healthy fish swim around cheerfully and do not crowd themselves into corners (exception: nocturnal fish and bottom-feeders like catfish).

• Sick fish have white spots, cotton-like deposits on their bodies, ragged fins, or dull skin (see Common Illnesses, page 38).

• Buy the fish one species at a time and not all at once (see Suggested Combinations, page 31).

Transporting the Fish

At the pet or aquarium store the fish is packed in a plastic bag, which is half filled with water. In addition, the bag is wrapped in newspaper for protection from the cold. Now it's time to take the fish home without delay. But be careful and don't shake the bag. Keep the package upright. This ensures that the water surface is larger, and more oxygen can get into the water. Then breathing is easier for the fish. Since being transported is a great stress for the fish, you should get them home as soon as possible.

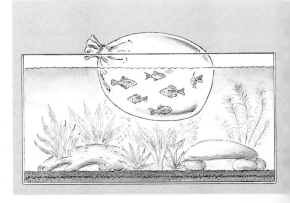

1. Lay the closed transporting bag on the surface of the water.

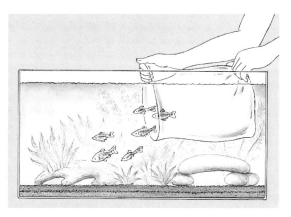

2. *The fish swim out of the bag into the aquarium. Don't tip the bag.*

Stocking the Tank
Drawings 1 and 2

Fish are cold-blooded animals (like lizards and snakes). They do not maintain a stable body temperature like humans do, but they adapt to the temperature around them. However, fish cannot adapt to sudden alterations of temperature from cold to warm or from warm to cold.

Water conditioners: Before you put the fish in the aquarium, add the water conditioner to the water. It protects the fishes' mucous membranes and makes getting acclimated easier.

From bag to aquarium: This is the correct way to put the fish in:
• To keep the fish from suffering any temperature shock, first lay the closed bag on the surface of the water (see drawing 1). After about 15 minutes, the water temperature in the bag has equalized to that of the aquarium.
• Carefully open the bag and hold it firmly with one hand. At the same time, use a glass to slowly pour the aquarium water into the bag until it's full.
• Slowly sink the bag horizontally into the water so the fish can swim out (see drawing 2). Never just tip the bag in. The fish should be able to move into the aquarium on their own and under no pressure.

The Perfect Water World
Drawings 3 and 4

With fish, the aquarium comes to life. Their lives—like our lives—depend essentially on oxygen. The plants see to it that there is always enough available.

Day: Fish breathe oxygen (O_2) in, carbon dioxide (CO_2) out. In photosynthesis (see Useful Terms, page 58) the plants take up carbon dioxide and give off oxygen (see drawing 3), which the fish use to breathe.

Night: In the darkness, the plants also breathe oxygen in and carbon dioxide out, like the fish (see drawing 4). Even though photosynthesis doesn't take place in the dark, the oxygen produced during the day is enough for the plants and the fish. Plants basically need only a little oxygen, and fish use considerably less during their night's rest than during the day.

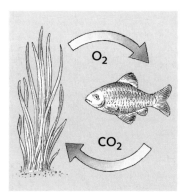

3. *By day: Plants give off oxygen to the fish, the fish give off carbon dioxide to the plants.*

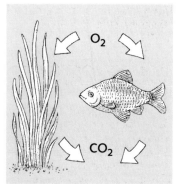

4. *By night: Fish and plants take in oxygen and give off carbon dioxide.*

The Most Popular Fish for Beginners

The fish are the stars in any aquarium. Not only are their shimmering colors fascinating, but their movements are also. It is a simple pleasure just to watch how easily and elegantly they glide through the water.

A life in the water: Fish are so well adapted to life in the water that they cannot survive on land. Every kind of fish lives in a certain depth of water, to which it is adapted to by shape. Thus, different species look entirely different from one another, depending on their differences or their water habitat.

The Ram is a very easily contented and easy-to-care-for fish that fits well in a community aquarium.

The Body Shape of the Fish

The shape of a fish indicates what kind of water it lives in. Some examples should clarify this:

• Fish found in fast-flowing water often have a sturdy, muscular, compressed forebody (Characin).

• Fish living in calm waters that are rich in plants are often compressed sideways and have a high back (Gouramis).

• Fish that live on the bottom often have a body that is flattened from upper to under side and have a flat belly (Armor-Plated Catfish).

• Fish with straight backs and back fins set way to the rear often swim just under the surface of the water (Egg-Laying Toothed Carps).

• Fish with cylindrical bodies chiefly move through the middle layers of water (Barbs).

The position of the mouth indicates how the fish feeds and in which area of the water it is active most of the time.

• Mouth upturned: The fish lives and feeds near the surface of the water (Guppy; see drawing, page 23).

• Mouth terminal: The fish inhabits the middle areas of the water and finds its food there (Tiger Barb; see drawing, page 23).

• Mouth underslung: Fish that live on the bottom mainly seek their food on or in the ground (Clown Loach; see drawing, page 23).

Why Can't Fish Laugh?

They don't need to.

They indicate their feelings toward their partners or express threats toward their rivals by the position of their fins, the placement of their body in relation to the other fish, and by changes in their color.

The Fins

Most fish have seven fins: one dorsal, caudal, and anal fin each, as well as two each of pectoral and ventral, or pelvic, fins. Some species (for example, Characins and some Catfish) have an additional small fin between the dorsal and caudal fins called the adipose fin. The fins move the fish forward or backward and hold it in a particular position. The caudal fin serves as the fish's motor, while the other fins are only used for steering.

The little Cardinal Tetra is strikingly colored and lives in a school.

 ### Why Does the Fish Move Its Fins When It Isn't Swimming?

Predatory fish, such as perch, which are lurking for prey, only move the pectoral fins and are otherwise almost motionless in the water. These fin movements are necessary so that they can stay in position in the water without being moved along by the current. When prey comes into sight, the predatory fish gives a swing of the caudal fin to attack.

The Swim Bladder

Many fish have a swim bladder (see drawing, page 22). It contains a mixture of gases, which changes according to whether the fish sinks or swims to the top. The swim bladder allows the fish to float in the water, climb to the top, or sink to the bottom.

Many fish that live on the bottom have a vestigial swim bladder. Some fish (for example, Bristle-Mouth Catfish) don't have any swim bladder at all. Fish without a swim bladder or with a rudimentary one can only move themselves upward with a very powerful thrash of the fins; otherwise they immediately sink to the bottom.

Sometimes a fish in water that is too cold gets a cold in its swim bladder. Then it can no longer move to the top without moving its fins.

How Do Fish Sleep?
Because fish don't have eyelids, it looks as though they never sleep. But that isn't so. When they want to rest, they withdraw to a quiet part of the aquarium. There they use less energy and then pass several motionless hours in a kind of sleep. Clown loaches are sometimes assumed to be dead because they "sleep" so soundly without moving at all. When in this state, they should not be "woken up."

The Lateral Line
The lateral line of the fish is a very special organ that functions something like radar. It runs along under the scales on both sides of the body as a straight, curving, or even dotted line from the head to the base of the tail. The lateral line perceives the finest movements and changes of current. So the fish perceives accurately if it is coming up to an obstruction or if an enemy is swimming toward it.

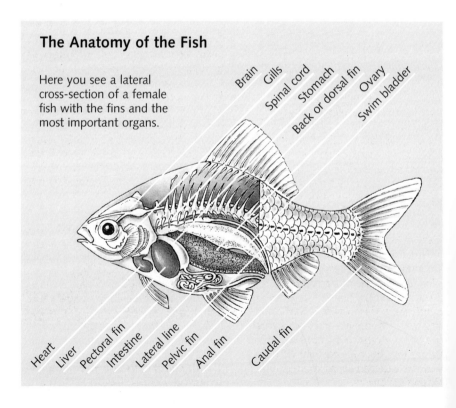

The Anatomy of the Fish

Here you see a lateral cross-section of a female fish with the fins and the most important organs.

Brain Gills Spinal cord Stomach Back or dorsal fin Ovary Swim bladder

Heart Liver Pectoral fin Intestine Lateral line Pelvic fin Anal fin Caudal fin

Why Don't Fish Bump into the Aquarium or Other Fish?

This also has to do with the lateral line. It enables the fish to feel when it swims up to an obstacle or when another fish approaches it. Even if the fish can't see anything at all (for instance, at night), it can nevertheless change its swimming direction in time to avoid a collision. Therefore fish that live in schools also never bump into one another.

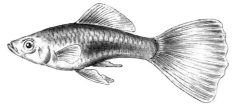

Guppy with upturned mouth.

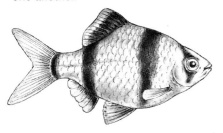

Tiger Barb with terminal mouth.

Are Fish Ticklish?

You would certainly not tickle your fish. But if you bang on the glass of the aquarium, the fish registers discomfort just as you do when you are tickled. This is because of its lateral line (see page 22), which perceives even gentle tremors immediately.

Fishes' Breathing

Fish don't breathe with their lungs like humans do, but with their gills. They draw water in through their mouth and force it past the gill leaflets, which are supplied with many blood vessels. From there—as in our lungs— the oxygen dissolved in the water passes into their bloodstream. The water is expelled again through the closing gill covers.

In addition, fish also take in oxygen through the skin—as do all other creatures, including humans. Therefore they often have difficulty breathing when they have mucous membrane injuries. But some species of fish have developed still other respiratory organs.

Labyrinth Fish (page 27) have rudimentary gills, but they also have the "labyrinth." This organ is located in the head behind the gills and has many fine branchings (hence the name). The fish takes up air and water on the surface and forces them both through the labyrinth. There the necessary oxygen is removed from the mixture.

Armored Catfish (see page 29) also have intestinal respiration, with which the air is compressed in the far end of the intestine. There the oxygen is transferred to the bloodstream.

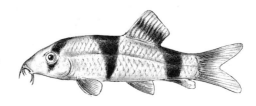

Clown Loach with underslung (or overshot) mouth.

A Swordtail pair

Golden-Eyed Dwarf Cichlid

Zebra Danios are school fish and are showy because

Red-Tailed Black Shark

A Clown Loach pair

A young Fantail

Fascinating Fish

of their blue-and-white stripes.

Lined Panchax

Golden Gourami

Glass Catfish

Easy-to-Care-for Fish

On the following pages I have put together a selection of fish that are especially easy to care for. They get along well with one another and do not have any very special demands as to aquarium and water quality. You can keep them well in a community tank at temperatures ranging from 75° to 79°F (24° to 26°C). As a rule, dried food is enough for their basic diet. But some fish also like treats too. These are listed under the Feeding instructions for each species. You will find any special care requirements under the Care instructions.

My suggested combinations (see page 31) offer you several different ways to combine various fish species.

The Latin Names of Fish

Each fish—like all other animals and plants—has a Latin name. It is helpful if you get familiar with them early on, since the Latin names are used consistently worldwide. When you know the Latin names, everyone knows precisely what fish is meant, even if the English name isn't given. The Latin name has two parts. The first part indicates the genus (comparable to people's last names), and the second part indicates the species (comparable to people's first names). A genus can have several species, but there are never two species with the same Latin name anywhere in the world.

Several closely related genera (the plural of genus) make up a family; several closely related families are collected into an order. So you can always tell which fish are closely related to one another and which are not.

Goldfish
Family Cyprinidae (Carps)

The Goldfish, with all its different forms and colors, is one of the best-known ornamental fish. It has been bred in China for almost 1,000 years. Besides the ordinary Goldfish there are also the Fantails, with doubled caudal fins, and quite a few other breeds. Over the course of years some special breeds like the so-called Bubble Eyes and Celestial have been developed. I recommend that you not attempt to keep these breeds at all, since they are susceptible to fungus diseases and, in my opinion, should not be bred anymore.

A notable feature of Goldfish is their slow change of color. The juvenile fish is black at first, then gets a golden-yellow abdomen. The gold turns to yellow, then to red. The last color to appear is white. If the fish is injured, the wound heals black and then slowly changes colors in the same order.

A female Goldfish can lay up to 3,000 eggs at once, which adhere to plants.

Size: Some Goldfish become up to 12 in (30 cm) long. You can only keep them as young fish in a 24-inch (60-cm) tank. Later you should put them in a garden pond or give them to an aquarist who has a bigger tank.

Care: You should keep Goldfish in an unheated aquarium (that is, at room temperature), and therefore not with the other fish mentioned in this book. The only exceptions are the Fantails (see photograph, page 25); they like a higher water temperature of 72° to 77°F (22° to 25°C). (Note Suggestion 5, page 31.)

Feeding: Ordinary flakes, plant flakes; no food sticks in the aquarium, since they are often hard to digest.

Live-Bearing Toothed Carp
Family Poecilidae of the Order Microcyprini (Small Carps)

The Live-Bearing Toothed Carps are among the most popular aquarium fish. They are not only very colorful but also robust and reproduce easily, so they are ideal fish for beginners. Males and females are easy to tell apart. The male is usually more slender and smaller than the female. In females the anal fin is round, whereas in the male it is pointed and changes into the sexual organ, the gonopodium. Also striking is the pregnancy spot on the rear body of the female. Here the fertilized eggs with the spawn in them show as a dark spot. In contrast to most other fish, these carps bring their young into the world live (see Birth Among Guppies, page 53). Depending on the species, it is often several hours before the young can swim properly.

Easy-to-care-for species: Among the best-known small carp species are the Guppy (*Poecilia reticulata*; see photograph, page 37), Molly (*Poecilia sphenops*; see photograph, page 33) Platy (*Xiphophorus maculatus*; see photographs, pages 16 and 32), Swordtails (*Xiphophorus helleri*; see photograph, page 24).

Size: Guppy 1 to 2¼ in. (3 to 6 cm); Molly 1½ to 2¼ in. (4 to 6 cm); Platy 1½ in. 56 to 2¾ in. (4 to 7 cm); Swordtail up to 5 in. (12 cm).

Care: Water temperature 68° to 86°F (20° to 30°C). Long-tailed species are delicate, since the ends of the fins do not have very much blood circulation. They thus are susceptible to fin rot and fungus infections.

Feeding: Varied feeding with flake food, algae, and gnat larvae. The females especially need animal protein, since they are often pregnant. Without proper food they quickly suffer from protein and mineral deficiencies and become thin and frail.

Threadfish or Labyrinth Fish
Family Anabantidae of the Order Perciformes (Perches)

Two "oddities" have led to both names of the Labyrinth Fish. They are called "Labyrinth Fish" because of the special respiratory organ, the labyrinth (see Useful Terms, page 58), and "threadfish" because their pectoral fins have developed into long sensory threads, or filaments. These threads enable them to more easily find their way in the dark waters of their habitat. The sexes are easy to tell apart. The females are usually rounder and have a lighter abdominal area. The males have pointed caudal and anal fins, which are round in the female. The colors change according to their mood. So males under attack often take on female coloration as camouflage. The reproduction of the labyrinth fish is remarkable. The males build compact bubble nests on the surface of the water (see Birth Among Fighting Fish, page 52), into which the eggs are spit and then guarded by the male.

Easy-to-care-for species: Siamese Fighting Fish (*Betta splendens*; see photograph, page 5); Dwarf Gourami

The smaller Tiger Barb male courts the larger female by repeatedly nudging her in the side.

(*Colisa lalia*; see photographs, pages 48 and 49); Blue Gourami (*Trichogaster trichopterus*), and Croaking Gourami (*Trichopsis vittatus*).

Size: Of the species named, 1½ to 2¼ in. (4 to 6 cm); Blue Gourami up to 4¾ in. (12 cm). Labyrinth Fish grow very quickly, but they seldom live longer than three years.

Care: Temperatures of 77° to 81°F (25° to 27°C). Regular water changes once a week is particularly important for Labyrinth Fish, since they are susceptible to ulcers and fungus diseases. The animals cannot tolerate any drafts across the aquarium. Two male Siamese Fighting Fish should never be kept in a 24-in. (60-cm) tank. Since there is only enough space for one male's territory, they will always fight bitterly to occupy the existing space.

Feeding: Dry food, with frozen food for variety.

Characins

Several families of the Order Characiformes (Characins)

Most Characins are school fish, which only feel safe and sound in a group. They are agile swimmers and often strikingly colored. The Characins are easily recognizable by the adipose fin at the base of the tail (see Fins, page 20). Telling the sexes apart is hard. Usually the females are rounder and less colorful than the males.

Easy-to-care-for species: Neon Tetra (*Paracheirodon innesi*), Cardinal Tetra (*Cheirodon axelrodi*; see photograph, page 21), Flame Tetra (*Hyphessobrycon flammeus*), Jewel Tetra (*Hyphessobrycon callistus*; see photograph, page 1), Black Tetra (*Gymnocorymbus ternetzi*), Emperor Tetra (*Nematobrycon palmeri*), Congo Tetra (*Phenacogrammus interruptus*; see photograph, page 29).

Size: The species named, 1½ to 2¼ in. (4 to 6 cm), although the Congo Tetra can grow up to 3½ in. (9 cm). Since it swims a great deal, it should only be kept in a 24-in (60-cm) tank as a young fish and later be transferred to a larger tank.

Care: Water temperature 73° to 81°F (23° to 27°C).

Feeding: Dry food; for treats, gnat larvae, freeze-dried or frozen with vitamins.

Barbs

Several families of the Order Cypriniformes (Carps)

Many Barbs have barbels on both sides of their mouth, which accounts for their name (Latin *barba* means "beard"). These serve as taste organs when the fish are searching for food on the bottom. Barbs are usually brightly colored and lively fish, which live in schools. Thus they are safer from enemies who would eat them. Often several species of Barb swim together in one school. Barbs often lay eggs in open water. An exception is the Harlequin Fish, which attach their eggs to the undersides of leaves.

Easy-to-care-for species: Rosy Barb (*Puntius conchonius*; see drawing, page 27), Sumatra or Tiger Barb (*Puntius tetrazona*), White Cloud Mountain Minnow, also called Poor Man's Neon (*Tanichthys albonubes*; see photograph, page 57), Zebra Danio (*Brachydanio rerio*; see photograph, page 24), Harlequin Fish (*Rasbora heteromorpha*). You should only buy Barb species in schools of three to five fish.

Size: Of the species named, 1½ to 3 in. (4 to 8 cm).

Care: Dense planting in the rear area of the aquarium and floating plants. Much open swimming area. White Cloud Mountain Minnows are most comfortable in an unheated aquarium at temperatures of 64° to 72°F (18° to 22°C).

Feeding: All the usual kinds of food.

Cichlids

Family Cichlidae of the Order
Perciformes (Perches)

Cichlids occupy territories in the aquarium and form permanent pairs. Common to all species is attentive care to the young (see page 54). Spawn and fry are zealously defended against enemies. The brood care of the Mouthbrooders (see page 55) is especially interesting to watch. The female takes the eggs in her mouth, broods them there until they hatch, and only then lets her young fry out when there are no predators lurking. When there is danger the fry always flee back into the mother's mouth.

Easy-to-care-for species: The Ram (*Papiliochromis* [formerly *Microgeophagus*] *ramirezi*; see photographs, pages 20 and C4; drawing, page 2), Golden-Eyed Dwarf Cichlid (*Nannacara anomala*; see photograph, page 24), Purple Cichlid (*Pelvicachromis pulcher*); see photographs, pages 17 and 29), Egyptian Mouthbrooder (*Pseudocrenilabrus multicolor*; see drawing, page 30).

Size: Of the species named, 2 to 4 in (5 to 10 cm).

Care: Water temperature 77° to 84°F (25° to 29°C). Every cichlid pair occupies a territory and needs their own cave into which they can retreat.

Feeding: Dry food; in addition, frozen food and vitamins. Cichlids are predators and eat everything that fits into their mouths, including young guppies, unfortunately.

Catfish

Several families of the Order
Siluriformes (Catfish)

Catfish are indigenous all over the world and live at all water depths. In the

Male Dwarf Gourami

Male Congo Tetra

Purple Cichlid female with fry

aquarium the Catfish usually make themselves useful as "garbage collectors" because—depending on the species—they eat algae and the remains of food. There are the most amazing forms among the Catfish. The Armored Catfish, the best-known aquarium Catfish, have backs armored with sturdy scales (see photographs, pages 13, 53, and 64). They are animals prepared to defend themselves, though they have hardly any enemies. Armored Catfish often live to be older than 15 years. The Glass Catfish is entirely transparent (see photograph, page 25). The Bristle-Mouth Catfish has only very small eyes. Its numerous "antennae" (see photograph, page 56) serve to orient it in cloudy waters. Another curiosity is the Upside-down Catfish (see photograph, page 45). As its name indicates, it usually swims upside down.

Easy-to-care-for species: The armored catfishes (*Corydoras* species) are robust; the Glass Catfish (*Kryptopterus bicirrhis*) is long-lived but always remains somewhat shy; the Bristle-Mouth Catfish, also called the Blue-Chin Catfish (*Ancistrus dolichopterus*) is outstanding as an algae eater; it searches on the bottom for algae on stones and leaves; the Upside-Down Catfish (*Synodontis nigriventris*).

Size: Of the species named, 1½ to 4 in. (4 to 10 cm).

Care: The species named are undemanding and robust fish. They need a place to hide, but they also must have open space on the bottom for rooting.

Feeding: Food tablets; frozen food for supplementary feeding.

Loaches

Family Cobitidae of the Order Cypriniformes (Carps)

Loaches like to stay on the bottom. Most species have an underslung mouth (see page 20). Thus they can easily look for food on the ground with their numerous barbels.

Easy-to-care-for species: Dwarf Loach (*Botia sidthimunki*; see drawing, page 7), Skunk Botia (*Botia morleti*). The Clown Loach (*Botia macracantha*; see photograph, page 24) and the Red-Tailed Black Shark, also called the Red-Tailed Labeo (*Labeo bicolor*; see photograph, page 24) are popular and easily cared-for fish. They can be kept well in a small tank as young fish. Later they must be transferred to a larger tank.

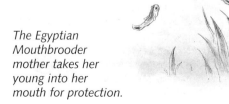

The Egyptian Mouthbrooder mother takes her young into her mouth for protection.

Size: Dwarf Loach and Skunk Botia 2¼ to 3½ in. (6 to 9 cm); Red-Tailed Black Shark and Clown Loach up to 6 in. (16 cm).

Care: Loaches are undemanding in regard to water quality but they need caves for hiding places.

Feeding: Food tablets.

Killifishes

Family Cyprinodontidae (Egg-Laying Toothed Carps) in the Order Microcyprini (Small Carps)

Killifishes are also known as Egg-Laying Toothed Carps. In nature they rarely live longer than six months. They are therefore also called seasonal fish, because in their natural habitats they hatch from their eggs during the rainy season, grow quickly, become sexually mature, spawn, and die. The eggs have a hard shell, which protects them from drying out for a long time—sometimes for even several years, when there is no rain. When it rains again, the rainwater weakens the shells and the fry hatch.

The Killifishes are very colorful (see the Lined Panchax, photograph, page 25). The females are frequently smaller and characteristically paler than the strongly colored males.

Easy-to-care-for species: Cape Lopez Lyretail (*Aphyosemion australe*), Aphyosemion striatum (*A. striatum*), Steel-blue Aphyosemion (*A. gardneri*).

Size: The species named become 2 to 3 in. (5 to 8 cm) in size.

Care: The water temperature should be between 70° and 73°F (21° and 23°C); Steel-blue Aphyosemions need warmer temperatures of 73° to 81°F (23° to 27°C). Killifishes don't have any great demands as to water quality. A dense planting is important, so they have enough places to hide.

Food: Dried food; freeze-dried and frozen food for supplementary feeding.

Suggested Combinations

3 to 10 days after conditioning
3 Siamese algae eaters, 1 Bristle-Mouth Catfish only with Suggestion 5 (see below)
1 algae eating suckermouth catfish

After another 7 days
Suggestion 1
7 Neon Tetras
5 Black Phantom Tetras (2 males, 3 females)
5 Harlequin Fish
2 Dwarf Gouramis (1 pair)
3 Armored Catfish
Suggestion 2
7 Zebra Danios
5 Tiger Barbs
3 Cherry Barbs
3 Armored Catfish
2 Purple Cichlids (1 pair)
Suggestion 3
7 Zebra Danios
7 Black Tetras
3 Armored Catfish
Suggestion 4
7 Black Neon Tetras
5 Jewel Tetras Red Phantom Tetras
Suggestion 5
3 small Fantails

After another 3 weeks
With suggestion 1
4 Guppies or Platys (2 pairs each)
With suggestion 2
4 Platys or Black Mollies (2 pairs each)
With suggestion 3
4 Platys, 4 Guppies, 2 Black Mollies (pairs of each)
With suggestion 4
3 Fighting Fish (1 male, 2 females) or 2 Rams (1 pair)

Proper Food and Feeding

Platys crowd around a food tablet. If you attach the tablet to the front wall of the aquarium, you can observe the fish at their meal.

Proper feeding is the most important thing in the care of an aquarium. It's no different for the fish than it is for you: They don't like to eat the same thing every day any more than you do. Since the fish can find hardly any natural food in the aquarium, with the exception of algae, variety in food is important. This isn't hard, for you can find plenty of foods available in the pet store to choose from. If you feed the fish monotonously, always with the same food, they can develop symptoms of deficiency and become sick. You can find out how to feed them properly on the HOW-TO pages 34 and 35.

Different kinds of food: Find out from your pet or aquarium store what the best food is for your pets. Some fish are plant eaters only; some are predators and need additional animal food. You can feed most fish with a good mixture of the different kinds of food.

Dry Food

Dry food is a mixture and contains everything that a fish needs. It is therefore good for the basic diet. Various types are for sale in the pet store.

Food flakes are sprinkled on top of the water. They float there and then slowly sink down. They are especially preferred by the fish in the upper and middle layers of water. There are flakes in various sizes, and there are purely vegetable flakes for plant eaters.

Food pellets or food sticks are little sticks of compressed dry food. They are best suited to larger fish.

Food tablets are ideal for bottom-dwelling fish, since the tablets quickly sink to the bottom of the aquarium. But there are also sticky tablets that can be fastened to the glass. These give you an especially good chance to observe the fish at their meals.

Granules, also called "food crumbs" are a very valuable feed. However, the fish don't always take to them immediately. You have to work regularly to train them to eat the granules. You'll succeed if you offer the granules alternately with food flakes at first. It often looks as if the fish don't like it. But that isn't so. They only need less of it because the food crumbs are very nourishing.

Frozen Food

Fish gladly accept frozen food as a change from dry food.

Frozen food is a good substitute for live food, for it consists of deep-frozen food animals, such as gnat larvae. It is shaped just like a bar of chocolate and must be kept in the freezer. Always break off only as much of the bar as you are going to give your fish at each feeding.

Freeze-dried food also consists of food animals that have been deep-frozen and dried. It is very good for supplementary food. As a rule the fish like it very much; it's a real treat for them.

Live food is usually available in the pet store as red or white gnat larvae. This would really be the most natural

Two Gold Dust Mollies wait impatiently for the next feeding.

food for your fish. But since it is often contaminated with pesticides and diseases, I advise against using it for feed. The best rearing food for your fry are brine shrimp. You can raise these yourself (see page 56) and then always be able to give fresh food to your fry.

Vitamins and Minerals

Vitamins and minerals are just as important for your fish as they are for you. Dry food contains too few of them. Therefore you should regularly add vitamins (from the pet store) to the water and put one vitamin drop on the frozen food daily.

HOW-TO:
Feeding Right

The two most important ground rules for your fishes' healthy diet are (1) that you feed with a lot of variety and (2) that you never overfeed. If you always follow these basic principles, your fish will stay fit and healthy for a long time.

How to Feed?
Drawings 1 and 2

Flakes, granules, and freeze-dried food are sprinkled through the feeding hole in the aquarium cover (see drawing 1) onto the surface of the water. The fish then swim up to the surface and eat up the flakes raining down on them.

Food tablets are simply allowed to sink to the bottom of the aquarium. There the bottom-feeding fish species can eat them (see drawing 2). You can also stick the tablets to the front glass. The great advantage to this is that you can then comfortably observe how much the fish eat of the tablet and when they need "resupplies."

Frozen food for smaller fish is dropped onto the water as a frozen cube with vitamins added. It then floats on the surface and thaws from the outside in. Red gnat larvae appear to move as they thaw. So they are eagerly eaten, especially by the predatory fish, which only react to the movement of the food. For large fish you must first

2. The fish eat from a food tablet lying on the bottom.

How Much to Feed?

Because it's so nice to see the hungry fish "begging" at the glass when you approach the aquarium, you will probably want to feed your fish often. But you should repress the urge, because it isn't at all good for the fish if they have too much to eat all the time. They will just become sluggish and easily susceptible to many possible diseases. At every feeding, you must be careful not to give your fish too much to eat.
• Only feed as much as your fish can eat within five minutes.

1. Flaked food is scattered over the surface of the water.

thaw the frozen food in a small dish with warm water. Otherwise they will swallow the still-frozen food whole and then may suffer from an upset stomach.

Live food, such as brine shrimp (Artemia), are always fed fresh out of the jar (see Raising Live Brine Shrimps, page 56). To do this, you tip the contents of the jar through the sieve and add only the brine shrimp, not the eggshells, to the aquarium.

The food should thus not sink farther than 2 in. (5 cm) under the surface of the water. Otherwise leftover food collects on the bottom and begins to get moldy and rot; this pollutes the water and thus also adversely affects the health of your fish.
• Divide the amount per feeding into several smaller portions.
• Feed daily. If you should ever not have time, it's better to miss a feeding altogether than to feed in a hurry or to ask some-

one who doesn't know how to do it right to take over. It doesn't hurt the fish to have nothing to eat for one day once in a while. Even in the wild they don't always get enough food. The only exceptions are young fish. They need food every day so that they can grow strong.

Feeding During Vacations
Drawing 3

If your aquarium is well cared for, you can leave it on its own for two to three weeks without any problem and go on vacation without any worries. Naturally you must see to it that your fish receive their food regularly. Of course, fish can go hungry for a couple of days, but if you are going to be away longer, you should have someone reliable take over the feedings for you.

Practicing feeding: If a friend or relative is going to do the feeding for you, you need to practice with your stand-in ahead of time. It's best if you show your replacement exactly how to feed. And it would cer-

The Seven Golden Rules of Feeding

1. Never feed if you don't have enough time. You should always watch your fish carefully as they eat. All fish should approach the food immediately and eat it all at once. If your fish don't eat, they are either still full from the last feeding or they are not well (see Recognizing and Treating Illnesses, page 36).

2. Always feed flakes first. Don't pulverize these (except for fry).

3. Feed the flakes in small portions so that they never sink more than 2 in. (5 cm) below the surface before they are eaten. Only feed while everything is being eaten immediately.

4. For "dessert" you can then give the fish some frozen or freeze-dried food.

5. Never feed when you have just turned on the light first thing in the morning. Your fish are only properly awake and able to take up the food 30 minutes later.

6. Never feed when you have just changed something in the aquarium (e.g., taken fish out or put new ones in, or changed the water). Before you put new fish in, always first feed the ones that are already in the aquarium.

7. Never turn off the filter to feed; the fish are used to the current.

tainly not be a bad idea if your substitute could feed a few times under your supervision before you go. I also suggest you put a note beside the aquarium on which the most important rules are listed once more. Then certainly nothing will go wrong.

Automatic feeder: You can, of course, also use an automatic feeder. There are various kinds of these. I have had the best experience with a feeder that you

simply fasten to the cover (see drawing 3). You can set the feeding times. Then the food falls through the feeding hole into the tank at the preset feeding times.

Tip: You should install the automatic feeder at least 14 days before you go away. Then you will see whether it functions reliably. At the same time you can determine the right size portions.

3. Practical for vacations: the automatic feeder.

Prevention and Cure of Illness

There's an old saying, "healthy and happy as a fish in water." Unfortunately this isn't always so, for your fish can get sick, too. While you can't always avoid illness, you should try to prevent an illness from breaking out.

The Ten Rules of Prevention

Prevention is always better than cure.

1. Always take good care of the filter (see page 44).

2. Promote plant variety and plant growth in the aquarium (see page 47).

3. Provide sufficient oxygen in the water through good plant care.

4. Buy sturdy, healthy fish that get along well with one another (see page 18).

5. Feed regularly, with plenty of variety, and never too much (see page 34).

6. Supplement food regularly with vitamins and minerals (see page 33).

7. Change water regularly, adding new preparations and water conditioners (see page 46).

8. Do not use cold water when changing water; to do so would cause dangerous drops in temperature (see page 46).

9. Only perform one maintenance task on the same day (see page 46).

10. Remove dead fish at once.

Recognizing and Treating Illnesses

You may notice first that all is not well with one of your fish while observing a feeding. If a fish has no desire to eat, it doesn't feel well either. But there

This catfish uses its sucker mouth to scrape the algae from the aquarium glass.

are still other signs of illness. These and the proper treatments are listed under the most common fish diseases (see page 38). Since illness can often break out in an aquarium like a wild fire, you must handle it quickly. The sooner you get started doing something, the better the chances of cure.

• Write down all behavior changes and signs of illness in your fish so that you can describe them as precisely as possible.

• Take this list to the pet dealer or veterinarian and get a medication.

• Clean the filter before you add the medication to the water.

• Follow the dosages given on the label exactly. They always depend on the water content. You can figure the number of gallons in the tank by using the following equation: Length of the tank times the width of the tank times the height of the tank, divided by 231 equals the number of gallons ($L \times W \times H \div 231$ = gallons).

• Never use medications and water preparation chemicals together, or the medication won't work right.

• Increase the oxygen content (see Airstones, page 7).

What Else You Can Do

To supplement treatments you can use the so-called "sauna method." This involves increasing the water temperature. Under warmer water conditions, the disease organisms multiply, the illness breaks out completely, and the medication can effectively combat all the disease organisms.

The most beautiful thing about the Guppies are their magnificently colored caudal fins.

How to go about it:
• Change a third of the water without adding any water preparations.
• Increase the temperature on two successive days by at most 4°F (2°C). The water temperature should not reach more than 90°F (32°C).
• Increase the oxygen content.
• Add medication as prescribed.

As a rule, the external signs of the illness are gone eight days after the beginning of treatment. Then the water temperature is again lowered and ordinary feeding and vitamins may resume.

After another eight days, change another third of the water, but this time add the water preparations.

After treatment with medications:
It may become necessary to filter the water over carbon (see page 7). Add the dry carbon filter in a filter pouch and cover with filter padding. This catches the carbon dust. The effect of the carbon lasts only one week. Then throw away the carbon. Do not reuse it!

Common Illnesses

You will notice when a fish is sick if it changes its behavior and/or it changes in appearance. You must do something about illness immediately. In the following disease scenarios I tell you how best to treat the ailing fish.

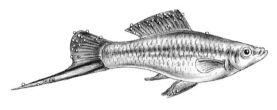

Swordtail with white spot disease

Illness Through Faulty Care

Scenario 1: Colors fade or change to the opposite (light colors become dark or vice versa); fish gasp for air at the water surface; fish make uncontrolled swimming motions, wobble, swirl around, or bump into the aquarium.
• Diagnosis: Chemical poisoning.
• Causes: Remnants of soaps in the bucket that is used for care of the aquarium; overfertilization of the aquarium plants; poisonous vapors that have gotten into the aquarium from the outside (e.g., hair spray or insecticides for house plants).
• Countermeasures: Total water change, with water preparations and mucous membrane protectors added. Do not feed the fish for two days. Check the filter. Watch the fish carefully. Since their resistance is weakened, other diseases may appear.
Scenario 2: Colors slowly fade; fish act quiet and swim slantingly to sideways; their eyes bulge and they breathe fast; the skin around the eyes gradually becomes dark.

• Diagnosis: Slow poisoning through bad water quality.
• Causes: During general cleaning of the aquarium, too many procedures carried out at once; wrong or poor-quality water (e.g., rainwater, well water) used for water change; gases given off by rotting matter on the bottom; improper decorations. Fish have mucous membrane injury.
• Countermeasures: Change a third of the water; increase the oxygen content; give appropriate medications; do not feed fish for three days.

Parasitic Illnesses

Scenario 3: Fish don't eat; they rock or twitch their fins. White dots appear at the borders of the fins, later all over the body.
• Diagnosis: White spot (see drawing above left).
• Cause: Infestation with parasites.
• Countermeasures: Kill the parasites with the appropriate medications. In addition, use the "sauna method" (see page 36).
Scenario 4: Dust-like dots, spots more yellowish than white (especially in Barbs and Killifish).
• Diagnosis: Velvet disease.
• Cause: Fungus infection.
• Countermeasures: Same as for white spot.
Scenario 5: Ulcers that break open; inflamed places with white borders (often in Labyrinth Fish and Goldfish).
• Diagnosis: Metabolic disturbance.

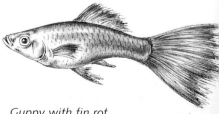

Guppy with fin rot

- Causes: Poor water value; parasitic infestation of wound edges.
- Countermeasures: Wash out the filter mass; change a third of the water; give appropriate medications.

Scenario 6: Fins become ragged and die back; color pales (often in Guppies and Fantails).
- Diagnosis: Fin rot (see drawing, page 38, bottom right).
- Causes: Injury in transport; oxygen deficiency; parasite attack.
- Countermeasures: Increase the oxygen content, change a third of the

Black Molly with mucous membrane fungus

water; wash out the filter mass; give appropriate medications; give vitamins.

Scenario 7: Fading color on back and tail; fish become white (in Characins and Barbs).
- Diagnosis: Neon disease.
- Cause: Parasite infestation.
- Countermeasures: Difficult to combat, but the spread of the parasites is inhibited with appropriate medications; supplement fishes' diet with vitamins.

Scenario 8: Cottony and moldlike deposits.
- Diagnosis: Fungus infection after injury to mucous membrane (see drawing, above).
- Cause: Physical injury destroys the mucous membrane, which is infected by fungus.

- Countermeasures: Change a third of the water; add appropriate medications; increase oxygen content; supplement with vitamins. After treatment, wash out filter mass.

Diseases Caused by Bacteria or Viruses

Scenario 9: Fish grow fatter and fatter, and threaten to burst; scales are raised (often in Fantails, Barbs, and Loaches).
- Diagnosis: Dropsy
- Causes: Bacterial or viral infection. Metabolic disturbance resulting from the wrong kind or too much food produces a similar appearance.
- Countermeasures: If possible, keep ailing fish in another tank. Stimulate metabolism with addition of salt; increase oxygen content and temperature; do not feed fish; give appropriate medications.

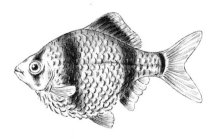

Tiger Barb with ascites (or dropsy).

Water Trumpet

Fanwort

The Java Fern is an undemanding and decorative plant.

Argentine Waterweed

Amazon Swordplant

Floating Fern

Suitable Aquarium Plants and Their Care

Plants play an important role in your aquarium. They are not only pretty decorations, but they also perform many important tasks at the same time.

What Are Plants Good For?

Plants supply oxygen, which fish—like humans and all other living creatures—need to breathe. This occurs during photosynthesis (see Useful Terms, page 58). In order for photosynthesis to occur, plants need light to use for energy. Therefore your aquarium must have light for 12 to 14 hours daily (see page 4). But providing oxygen is not all the plants do during photosynthesis. They also remove from the water the carbon dioxide that the fish exhale. A regular exchange of oxygen and carbon dioxide occurs between the fish and the plants (see The Perfect Water World, page 19).

Plants purify the water of substances that are poisonous for the fish. For example, the plants use nitrogren to grow. Fish give this out with their excretions. In time this nitrogen would poison the aquarium water, but the plants ensure that this never happens. They take up the nitrogen with their leaves or their roots and so remove it from the water. Thus they contribute essentially to healthy aquarium water.

Plants offer cover so that the fish can hide in the foliage of the plants if they ever want to withdraw and have their peace and quiet. Newly introduced fish can hide between the plants and observe their new surroundings.

Young fish are safer from predators among the plants. Plants also form boundaries to mark territories. And they offer shade for fish, which do not always like to swim in bright light.

Plants serve as places to lay eggs. Many fish have a preference for particular plants, usually finely branched ones, during their spawning time. Without these plants in the aquarium, the stimulus for the fish to spawn is absent. Thus if you ever want to breed fish, you must get to know exactly which plants your fish prefer. Find out from the pet dealer, who will certainly be able to help you and give you some good tips.

Can Fish Suffocate?

Only Labyrinth Fish can actually suffocate. Since their gills have atrophied, they mainly breathe air at the surface of the water through their labyrinth (see Useful Terms, page 58). If they are prevented from getting to the surface, they can suffocate. But the other fish also need sufficient oxygen in the water to be able to breathe easily. The plants provide for this. And you must thus make sure that there are many plants in your aquarium and that these grow well.

What Do Plants Need?

For the plants to grow well in the aquarium they need optimum conditions:
- Bottom material in which the roots can find a foothold (see page 8).
- Light, 12 to 14 hours daily, to be

Plants are very important in the aquarium. They offer oxygen, remove the carbon dioxide exhaled by the fish, and help to recycle the waste products.

able to carry on enough photosynthesis (see page 4).

• Enough nutrients through regular fertilization (see page 47), especially iron and nitrogen.

• Enough carbon dioxide for photosynthesis (see Useful Terms, page 58). The more carbon dioxide plants have available, the better they can process the surplus nitrogen in the aquarium from the wastes produced by the fish.

• Mild water circulation through the filter so that nutrients and carbon dioxide in the tank are evenly·distributed (see Filter, page 6).

• Regular pruning of fast-growing plants, which otherwise overgrow the others (see Plant Care, page 47).

Easy-to-Care-for Plants

Like the fish, the plants must also fit in with each other and have the same requirements for tank size and water temperature. You can put all the plants on my plant suggestion list (see page 15) in your aquarium without any difficulty. Here are descriptions of still more plants that are good for your aquarium, and some tips on how best to mix them.

Rosette-forming Plants

This group includes all plants whose leaves grow out of one spot, like a kind of rosette.

Cryptocorynes (Water Trumpet; see photograph, page 40): These have a sturdy yellow or blue flower cup, which is often raised over the surface of the water. Cryptocorynes propagate themselves in the aquarium by means of offshoots (see Useful Terms, page 58) in the soil. First they form roots, then leaves. All cryptocorynes have very sensitive roots. Therefore you must be care-

ful when planting them not to crush the roots with your fingers (see Putting in the Plants, page 15).

Sagittaria (arrowhead) and *Vallisneria* (tapegrass): These are very similar to cryptocorynes in their propagation and care. Sagittarias also grow at lower temperatures and are therefore suitable for Goldfish aquariums.

Echinodorus species (Amazon Swordplant): In the wild they are mostly found alone. They are very decorative and good in the aquarium for single plantings (for example, the red Amazon swordplant; see photograph, page 40). They propagate through offshoots. These are long stems that usually rise above the mother plant and often grow right out of the water. First the leaf develops on this stem and later the roots. Numerous flowers and daughter plants develop on the offshoot at the same time. The mother plant is often so weakened by this that it dies. Regular fertilization with nitrogen and iron is therefore especially important for the *Echinodorus* species (see Plant Care, page 47).

Tip: As soon as an offshoot develops, cut it back to about two eyes, counting from the mother plant. The eyes are the places on the stem from which the flowers or the daughter plants form.

Anubias Species

These plants (see drawing below) are attractive, undemanding, and grow well where other plants are hogging the light. Their root form is the rhizome (see Useful Terms, page 59), which grows by creeping and always grows a leaf first and then the roots. Propagation is simple. Divide the plant with a knife and fasten the cut-off piece between two stones or tie it to a root. It will start growing immediately.

However, you should never plant it in the gravel because then the roots will begin to rot. Anubias are outstanding for single plantings if, for example, you bind the plant to a piece of driftwood with a nylon thread.

Stem Plants

These include all plants whose leaves occur on a stem, that is, do not grow out of one spot (e.g., the Argentine Waterweed and the Fanwort; see photographs, page 40). The growth nodules on the stem are able to develop flowers and offshoots as well as put out side shoots and white roots, which are also called air roots. Stem plants must be cut back regularly. They are easy to propagate. You only need to shorten them the way I describe on page 47.

Ferns

Like all ferns, aquarium ferns (e.g., the Java Fern; see photograph, page 40) are easy to recognize because the youngest leaf is rolled up like a snail and it only unrolls as the plant grows. Ferns reproduce very easily. The young plants develop on the undersides of the leaves of the mother plants. Black spots on fern leaves are normal in older leaves; the young plants form there. Even pieces of fern leaf without roots can develop complete new plants.

Floating Plants

This group includes plants that mostly live on the surface of the water, without rooting firmly. Some ferns, for example the Floating Fern, are floating plants. In the aquarium they cast a strong shadow and so prevent bushy plant growth from developing in the lower layers of the water. Ferns that float are also good for fish that build bubble nests (see Useful Terms, page 59) and provide hiding places for surface fish. If you are not keeping any of these fish species in your aquarium, you had better avoid floating plants.

Plastic Plants

Although many people might argue that plastic plants have no place in a "real" aquarium, the decision as to whether or not to use them depends on how involved a person plans to get with the aquarium. Almost all plastic plants available in pet stores today are safe and colorfast.

Should you decide to go with the plastic plants, follow the instructions on pages 14 to 15 regarding the placement of the different size plants. In addition, try to stay with natural-looking colors (e.g., brown, red, and green), especially if you are planning to keep very colorful fish in your aquarium.

The Anubias is a decorative and easy-to-care-for water plant.

Care of the Aquarium

The Rosy Barbs receive their name from their brilliant red coloring. The effect is especially beautiful in a densely planted aquarium.

The Water Environment

For humans, the air is the element in which we live; but for fish it's the water. Just as we prefer to breathe fresh, clean air, the fish want to swim in fresh, pure water. Only then do they keep healthy and feel comfortable. For your aquarium always to contain "good" water, it must be cleaned regularly. The most important requirements for the aquarium water are:

- Enough oxygen,
- enough carbon dioxide,
- small quantities of waste products, and
- few algae and snails.

Providing Oxygen

All living things—humans, animals, and plants—need oxygen to breathe. Oxygen is contained in the air and in the water. In the aquarium the fish take in oxygen from the water in the tank. The filter and ground bacteria need oxygen as well, which they use for the breakdown of waste materials (see Filter Care, right).

There must always be enough oxygen present in the aquarium water for the fish to survive and the bacteria to always "work" well. You achieve this with a dense planting (see What Are Plants Good For?, page 41).

Care tip: The plants must be fertilized regularly and the fast-growing species cut back at the proper time so they don't crowd out the other, more slowly growing species (see Plant Care, page 47).

Providing Additional Carbon Dioxide

Carbon dioxide is generated by the breathing of the fish and the activity of the filter and ground bacteria. It is an important nutrient for the plants. They need it in large quantities for photosynthesis (see Useful Terms, page 58).

Care tip: You can provide the plants with enough carbon dioxide with a CO_2 diffuser (see page 7).

Filter Care

In every aquarium, even when it is carefully looked after, there gradually develops a build-up of dirt from excrement, food remains, and decaying animal and plant parts. This "garbage," which is poisonous to the fish, is "eaten" by various helpers—the bacteria in the filter, in the ground, and in the water—and turned into harmless substances. Some of these substances are then taken up by the plants and recycled as nutrients (for example, nitrogen and carbon dioxide).

The bacteria that have settled in the foam in the filter (see Filter Materials, page 7), break down the dirt that is drawn in. However, this only works when the filter is cleaned regularly.

Care tip: About every four weeks you must wash out the foam material with lukewarm (never boiling hot) water. Do not use cleaners to do this; they will kill the bacteria. Finally, squeeze out the foam and use it over again. You only need to replace it when it changes its shape.

The Upside-Down Catfish searches a piece of wood for something edible.

Combatting Algae

Algae belong in an aquarium along with fish and plants. You should just make sure that the algae don't get the upper hand. Algae only multiply rapidly when the plants can't completely use the nutrients that are produced by the bacteria.

Care tip: Biological algae control is best for your aquarium. If you provide your plants with the optimal nutrients (see Fertilizing, page 47), the plants will overtake the algae in growth and take the nutrients away from them. With less nutrients available to them, the algae don't grow so vigorously. In addition you should have so-called algae eaters living in your aquarium. These are fish species that chiefly feed on algae. They control the algae growth so well that it is no longer a problem. I recommend the Bristle-Mouth Catfish and other similar species (see Suggested Combinations, page 31).

HOW-TO: Proper Care

The care of your aquarium is not time consuming if you do the necessary work regularly. However, you must always do only one of the jobs described here on the same day, or the stress is too much for the fish.

Important note: Always unplug the electricity before undertaking any cleaning task.

Changing the Water
Drawing 1

You should change one-third of the water every week (not more, or the quality of the water will change too much). The simplest way is to let the water out of the aquarium into a bucket with a siphon and hose.

Siphoning off the water: Place the bucket on the floor next to the aquarium. This difference in height is important; otherwise the water siphon won't function. Then fill the hose (see Shopping List, page 11) with water from the tap and hold both ends closed with your thumbs. Put one end of the hose in the aquarium and the other in the bucket, still holding both ends closed. First take your thumb off the hose end in the aquarium, then take your thumb from the hose end in the pail. The water will immediately start running into the bucket. If you hold the end of the hose close to the bottom of the aquarium and draw it across it, the siphon will also suck up remains of food, mulm, and algae. You should always keep your hand ready to close the hose end in the pail immediately if a fish should come too close to the suction of the hose. The fish can then swim away again. If a fish is sucked up, catch it in the bucket with a fish net and put it back in the tank.

Replacing the water: Tip out the water that has been siphoned off and replace it with the same quantity of lukewarm tap water (see Adding Water,

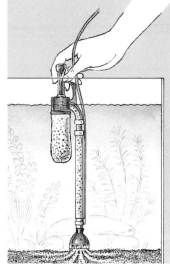

2. Move the mulm vacuum over the gravel carefully so as not to injure plant roots.

page 14). Add water preparations and water conditioner.

Siphoning Off the Mulm
Drawing 2

Once a week you should remove the mulm. You can simply siphon it off with the hose while you are changing the water (see Changing the Water, left).

At the pet shop you can also buy a mulm vacuum that is driven by an air pump (see page 7). It operates on the same principle as a vacuum cleaner. Carefully run the mulm vacuum back and forth over the gravel. Don't press too hard on the bottom while you're doing this or you will disturb the fine root network of the plants. Finally, rinse out the mulm vacuum's collecting bag.

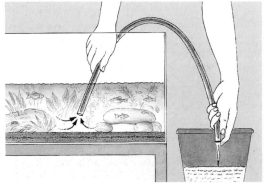

1. Siphoning off the water is very simple with a hose and a pail.

3. The algae growth on the glass is easily removed with the blade cleaner.

Cleaning the Walls
Drawing 3

The aquarium walls should be cleaned once a week. Wipe the glass on the outside with a damp cloth. You can clean the insides with an algae magnet or a blade cleaner (see Other Equipment, page 10).

The algae magnet consists of two magnets. The one with the "polishing coating" is fastened to the glass on the inside, the other held against it on the outside. When the outer magnet is moved, the inside magnet moves along with it and shaves the algae from the glass.

The blade cleaner is a scraper on a handle that holds a razor blade (see drawing 3). The algae are scraped away by the blade.

Plant Care
Drawing 4

Fertilizing: The most important fertilizers are iron and nitrogen. The plants need iron to form chlorophyll and nitrogen to develop leaves.
• Use the fertilizer exactly according to the directions on the package.
• Fertilize with liquid fertilizer after every water change.
• Place iron tablets on the gravel. Sink nitrogen tablets in the gravel next to the plants when they aren't developing pretty leaves anymore.
• Maintain a good supply of carbon dioxide (see CO_2 Diffuser, page 7).

Pruning stem plants: With the proper care, stem plants grow so lushly that they must be cut back regularly. As soon as a plant begins to grow along the top of the water, it's time for a pruning.
• Cut off two-thirds of the stem with a pair of scissors. After two weeks the plant will put out new shoots and now grow bushier.
• You can replant the cut-off stems. To do this, lay the stem

4. Weight cut-off stems with a stone. They will soon put out new roots.

flat on the gravel and anchor with a stone. Soon new roots will appear.

Other jobs: Remove one-half of each floating plant every three months. Pick off any parts of plants that have died; remove loose leaves from the aquarium.

Schedule for Regularly Occurring Jobs

Daily: Observe the appearance and behavior of the fish; check the temperature; check the equipment to be sure it's functioning; add carbon dioxide.

Weekly: Change one-third of the water, removing mulm and loose leaves at the same time; add water preparations with mucous membrane protector; clean the glass walls; place one iron fertilizer tablet in the back area of the aquarium.

Monthly: Cut back plants; clean filter (see page 44).

Semiannually: Change the fluorescent light bulb since its output decreases after a time.

As necessary: Vacuum up remains of food; remove dead leaves; take out dead fish; collect snails.

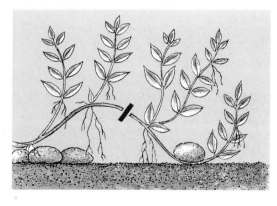

The Dwarf Gourami male (right) courts a female.

Keeping Snails Under Control

You may introduce snails with the plants in your aquarium, since usually there will be some snail spawn stuck to them. But this doesn't matter, for snails are useful as "garbage collectors." They eat the remains of food, died-off plant material, algae, and dead fish. They just shouldn't get the upper hand.

Care tip: When you have too many snails in the aquarium, you must remove them. The easiest way to do it is to set up a kind of "snail trap." First you feed your fish, and then you lay one to two food tablets on a flat stone. After some time there will be more and more snails collected there feeding on the tablets. You need only to gather up the snails and remove them.

The Aquarium During Vacations

When you have a substitute: It's easiest if you know someone who can take over the care of your aquarium while you are away on vacation. Make it as easy as possible for your friend.

• Practice every possible maneuver with your substitute and especially show her or him how to feed correctly.

• Write down the most important tasks on a list and put the reminder list next to the aquarium. Leave the address and telephone number of where you are going to be and also those of your pet store dealer, to whom your substitute can turn for help.

Tip: It's best to take care of the aquarium with your stand-in for the last few days before you leave on your vacation. Then you can answer all questions and your friend has a chance to get familiar with all the jobs.

When you don't have a substitute: If you don't know anyone to care for your aquarium responsibly while you are away, you can confidently leave it alone for two to three weeks. But then you should prepare the aquarium accordingly:

• Don't put any new fish in for several weeks before you go away. Otherwise you have no control over any diseases that might be introduced.
• Install the automatic feeder two weeks before you leave. Then feeding can continue automatically (see page 35).
• In the week prior to your departure, check the technical equipment every day to be sure it's functioning.
• Wash out the sponge of the filter three days before you leave (see Filter Care, page 44).
• Change one-third of the water two days before leaving, and at the same time siphon the mulm out of the tank. Add the preparations to the fresh water (see page 46).

First Aid for Deficient Water Quality

If you neglect your aquarium for a long time, the water quality can deteriorate. This can be life-threatening for your fish. At first, of course, you won't even notice any signs of malaise in your fish. As long as they have enough oxygen in the water, nothing happens. However, the smallest change (e.g., with the filter cleaning or a water change) may suddenly turn into a "catastrophe": Clear symptoms of poisoning appear in the fish.

Signs: You can recognize that the health of your fish is threatened by the following signs.
• The fish hover just under the surface of the water and breathe hard;
• they gasp for air;
• they refuse food;
• they show an inability to balance.

Now you have to act fast. You have to perform "first aid" if you want to save your fish.

Emergency first aid program: You must carry out the following measures faithfully for two to three weeks or they will not be successful.
• Carefully loosen the bottom materials with your fingers so that any trapped gases can escape. But don't stir up the bottom as you do it.
• Immediately (and then once a week) change one-third of the water. Put back less water, so that the surface of the water is about 2 in. (5 cm) lower than normal.
• Immediately (and then again after 14 days) clean the filter.
• Add constant oxygen with an airstone (see page 7). It's bad for the plants, of course, because the carbon dioxide is driven out of the water, but your fish are more important now.
• Add the appropriate medications and vitamins from the pet store to the water.

Mating takes place under the bubble nest.

• Do not feed for at least one day; on the second day, only feed a few flakes, no frozen food.

Don't resume normal care again until after three weeks. But every day observe your aquarium carefully to see if all the fish are eating normally. It can happen that one or more fish and some plants will not survive the emergency program. You must immediately remove dead fish and plants from the aquarium.

Tip: The best thing is not to let matters get this far. If you always clean your aquarium regularly and carefully, you will never have to undertake the emergency program. It's best if you follow the care schedule (see page 47); then you always know which tasks have to be done in the aquarium.

Mistakes and Mishaps

Sometimes a mistake happens or a mishap occurs. Here I list the main mistakes and mishaps and tell you how you can remedy them yourself.

When the Fish Refuse Food

Case 1: The fish take the food in, but they spit it right out again. The fish are full. Let them go hungry for two to three days.

Case 2: Fish don't approach the food but swim slowly or remain dully in the corner. Probably the water temperature is too low. Check the heater; possibly the element isn't in the water. If the heater is defective, change it. Put the new heater in the water and set it for the current water temperature and then every two hours raise it 4°F (2°C). The fish have to get used to the proper temperature slowly. Under no circumstances pour warm water into the aquarium.

When Cleaning Materials Get Into the Aquarium from the Water Bucket

Turn off the filter immediately, change all the water, and add the water preparations. Increase the oxygen content, which makes it easier for the fish to breathe. Put carbon in the filter and filter over carbon for three days. Then replace the foam in the filter with a new one and "inoculate" with a fresh bacteria culture from the pet store.

When the Lighting Setting Is Wrong

Case 1: Leaves of the plants "lean" on the stem. Reset the timer. Add iron fertilizer, raise the carbon dioxide content. After three to four days the plants should again appear normal.

Case 2: Leaves of the plants become narrow, transparent, and hard. Reset the timer. After five to six days the plants develop new, "normal" leaves. Then add iron fertilizer and increase the carbon dioxide content (see CO_2 Diffuser, page 7). After three weeks cut back the plants (see page 47).

When All the Fish Swim at the Water Surface

Case 1: The fish are breathing very fast. Immediately increase the oxygen content. Check the heater to see if it's working. If not, take it to the pet store. Get a replacement heater.

Case 2: The water smells different than usual. Check the filter to see if it's still letting enough water through. If not, clean the filter material. Change one-third of the water, removing mulm and remains of food when you do so (see page 46), and add water preparations to the fresh water. Do not feed the fish for three days.

When the Electricity Fails

Unplug everything—there could be a faulty piece of equipment. Check the fuses with an adult. Check all equipment to see if it is still working; replace faulty equipment. Increase the oxygen content. Do not feed the fish for two or three days.

When the Filter Stops Running

Pull the plug, clean the filter, and wash the motor through with water several times. If the filter still will not run, take the entire filter to the pet store dealer and have them check it there. Take the warranty and the sales slip with you. Perhaps you will be given a loaner until your filter is checked over. In the meantime, do not feed the fish and turn off the heater (only in a heated room). The aquarium temperature will drop somewhat, which won't disturb the fish much more, however. Carefully increase the oxygen content.

When the Water Temperature Is Too High

In midsummer, when it's very hot, you should try to keep your room dark by pulling the blinds or curtains. Otherwise you can only wait until the water temperature drops by itself. Carefully increase the oxygen content.

When the Aquarium Is Leaking

Mark with a marker where the aquarium leaks. Empty the aquarium, transfer fish and plants to a tub, and cover it with a cloth. Don't feed the fish. Adding oxygen with a airstone is important. Take the aquarium to the pet store, along with your warranty and sales slip, and leave it there for inspection. Perhaps in the meantime the pet store will lend you another aquarium. When setting up the aquarium again, you need to condition it the same as you did in the beginning (see HOW-TO: Setting Up, pages 14 and 15).

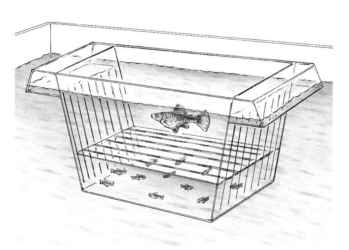

The guppy tank floats in the aquarium. The separating grill protects the young fry from being eaten by their own mother.

Observing and Experimenting

There are a whole lot of interesting things to see in an aquarium. In this chapter you will find a few directions for all the things you can explore and observe. I also give some tips for experimenting. In addition, there is also a suggestion for something you can make to help you observe the small fish in your aquarium.

A nyone who takes a little time can discover and observe much in an aquarium. The better you know the fish and their behavior, the more fun it is to take care of them.

How Fish Give Birth

One of the most exciting experiences in an aquarium is the birth of fish. Normally baby fish hatch from eggs (see Birth Among Fighting Fish, right). But there are fish that bring their young into the world live. They are therefore called "live-bearing." Guppies are among these.

Birth Among Guppies

Guppies reproduce very easily, so they are very good for observing how fish give birth.

What you need: To get everything started just right from the beginning, place a so-called "guppy tank" (from the pet store) in your aquarium. This is a special brooding tank with a separating grill in the bottom (see drawing, page 51). In the top section, place a pregnant female Guppy. You can tell she is pregnant by the pregnancy spot on the rear of her body. The eggs with the young in them are outlined in this spot.

What you can observe: At birth among the live-bearing fish, the egg membrane bursts at the moment in which the eggs are "born" into open water. The miniscule fish sink through the separating grid into the lower part of the brooding tank. They are only able to swim after about one hour. The separating grid is important, for it separates the fry from the mother fish. She doesn't care about the fry and would only eat them. As soon as the mother fish no longer has any dark spot visible on her abdomen, net her out and put her back in the ordinary aquarium. The fry are still kept in the guppy tank.

Setting up a rearing tank: Instead of a guppy tank, you can also let the female spawn in a rearing or nursery tank (see drawing, page 54). Then you separate the female from the young with a plate of glass that you place in the tank. This way you protect the fry from being eaten by their mother. In the fry's section you insert a foam filter and a airstone, which are both driven by an oxygen pump (see page 7).

Birth Among Fighting Fish

An entirely "ordinary" but no less exciting fish birth can be seen among the Fighting Fish. For this you must set up a second, smaller aquarium as a rearing tank.

What you need for it: One small aquarium with a volume of 30 qt (30 L), one cover with a light, one small air pump, one small foam filter, one 50-watt timed heater, one stick-on thermometer, and two bags of gravel (size 2 to 3 mm). For plants I recommend: one Floating Fern as a floating plant, one pot or bag of Green

Emerald Catfish rummage around for remnants of food on the aquarium bottom.

Ludwigia or Indian Water Friend, one stem Indian Water Star.

Setting up the rearing tank: You need to arrange the rearing tank exactly like your big aquarium (see HOW-TO, pages 14 and 15). However, don't place any decorations at all on the gravel, and don't add any fertilizer for the plants. The water temperature should be around 79°F (26°C).

Buying fish: Seven days after you have set up your rearing tank, buy two to three young female Fighting Fish, which you put in the rearing tank (see HOW-TO Buying the Fish, pages 18 and 19). You feed the females for four weeks with a varied diet of red gnat larvae, flakes, and vitamins, until they are really healthy (see HOW-TO: Feeding Right, pages 34 and 35). After four weeks you add a completely mature male Fighting Fish to the aquarium.

Make sure that the male is nice and large and doesn't have fins that are too long, or he may possibly already be too old to breed. Now increase the water temperature about 2°F (1°C) per day until it has reached 86°F (30°C).

Now it gets exciting: Within six to eight hours the male will build a large bubble nest at the water's surface and seek out one of the females. Now you had better take out the other females and put them in the large aquarium. Take a lot of time to observe during the next few days. You will see how the eggs fall to the bottom and are fertilized by the male. He collects all the eggs with loving care and spits them into the bubble nest one by one. You can count them there. Soon you will see how the young hatch. The father cares for them until they are able to swim on their own. Until then he keeps "repairing" the bubble nest so that the young don't fall out. Then the father's brooding drive is over. You'd better catch him and remove him now or he will eat his young. These remain in the rearing tank for the time being.

Birth Among Dwarf Gouramis

With Dwarf Gouramis it is easy to observe how the young fish slowly develop into adult fish.

What you need: The same equipment as for the breeding of Fighting Fish (see page 52).

What you can observe: Keep two Dwarf Gourami pairs in a rearing tank. Each pair builds a bubble nest into which the eggs are spit. This is the only service the parents provide for their young. Then they don't care about them anymore. Therefore you should take the parents out of the rearing tank. When the young fish hatch from the eggs, they are about (2 mm) in size. They can swim immediately. But if you look at them carefully, you'll notice that they are swimming on their backs and are borne by a fat bladder. This fat

bladder is a brilliant yellow spot, which looks like an egg yolk. And in fact, the first few days the fry do get their nourishment from the fat bladder and grow to about double their size on it. As soon as the fat bladder is used up, the little fish turn on their bellies and swim "properly." Now you must take over their feeding. It's best if you feed them with brine shrimp you have raised yourself (see page 56).

Brood Care Among Fish

You have now seen how fish fry come into the world. Many fish are no longer interested in their fry after they are born; in fact, they even eat them if you don't separate the young from the parents. But there are also other kinds of fish that care for their young very attentively. This behavior is called "engaging in brood care," and the mother and the father perform specific tasks. You can observe this if you raise the type of fish that care for their young.

Brood Care Among Purple Cichlids

These fish live like a regular family. If you breed them, you can observe the brooding behavior well.

What you need: You need the same equipment as for breeding Fighting Fish (see page 52). In addition you need one small piece of

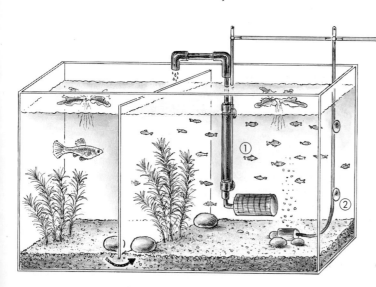

Breeding tank with foam filter ① and airstone ②. A glass plate installed in the tank separates the Guppy mother from her fry.

wood, three stones 2 to 3 in. (5 to 7 cm) in size, and one clay or pottery cave. For plants I recommend one Floating Fern as a floating plant, one potted Java Fern, one potted Dwarf Anubias, one bunch of Java Moss, and one bundle of Green Ludwigia. Arrange the rearing tank just the same as for the Fighting Fish (see page 52).

What you can observe: If the female has developed enough eggs in her body, it will show in her brilliant red abdominal spot. The male then swims almost on his side, lying diagonally in front of the female. He thus shows his dark egg spot on his spread dorsal fins. This means something like "Come with me and let's start a family." The male lures the female into the cave. There the female attaches her eggs to the roof of the cave. Then they are fertilized by the male. After about 36 hours, 200 to 300 young fish hatch out. They form a school and are cared for by both the father and the mother. The father's job is to carefully watch over the fry. He will attack any other fish that come too close to his offspring. The mother feeds the fry in front of the cave and shows them where they can find something to eat.

When the parents can no longer keep the school together, you can take them out. The fry are now independent.

Brood Care Among Egyptian Mouthbrooders

Among the mouthbrooders, brood care goes even further. You will be amazed what the fish have "thought out" to protect their young.

What you need: The same equipment as for breeding Fighting Fish (see page 52).

What you can observe: The male, swimming on his side, invites the female with the trembling of his fins into a previously dug out hollow in the gravel, which is usually located between two pebbles. Then the male lays himself flat. This means something like, "This is the right place, this is where I would like you to lay the eggs so that I can fertilize them." The female then lays her eggs in the hole, and the male fertilizes the eggs with strong trembling (with all his fins). Since the future father does not help with care of the young, you should then take him out of the rearing tank.

Now it gets exciting: At first it looks as though the female is eating the fertilized eggs. She takes them into her mouth and holds them there. In the next 10 days you will observe that the female's head keeps getting larger, but her body appears to get smaller. After about 10 days about 50 fry hatch unnoticed in the mouth of the mother. You only see them when the mother lets them out in a quiet corner of the aquarium for the first time. The fry always stay near the opening of her mouth. For about eight days they always flee into their mother's mouth at the least sign of danger (see drawing, page 30). In this way they are protected from any possible predator.

Raising Brine Shrimp

The best way to feed your fish fry is with brine shrimp (Latin *Artemia*), which you can raise yourself.

What you need: 3 clear, transparent 24-oz. (0.75-L) glass bottles; 3 corks to fit them, each with two holes in it; 1 valve (see Air Valves, page 8); 3 pieces of air hose each about 2¾ in (70 cm) long; 1 air pump; 3 airstones that will fit through the bottle necks; 1 package of sea salt (no iodized salt); artemia eggs and 1 artemia net (all from the pet store).

How to do it: Put the three bottles next to each other in the vicinity of the heating unit, since brine shrimp can only hatch at a water temperature of 79°F (26°C). Put one of the airstones in each bottle, each with a piece of hose attached. Attach one of the free hose ends to the valve, which is connected to the air pump, with the strength of the air current adjusted. Put the other free hose ends through the open holes in the corks of the next two bottles so that they are about about ¾ in (2 cm) into the bottle. Thus the water pressure is transferred from one bottle through the hose and directed to the airstone in the next bottle. In the last bottle the excess pressure is released through the open hole in the cork. Since you always need only a few freshly hatched brine shrimp, always start just one bottle per day. Fill it with 16 fl. oz. (0.5 L) luke-warm water, 1 oz. (30 g) salt (this gives a salt concentration of 6% and is like seawater), and the artemia eggs. Use the valve to let enough air into the bottle so that the eggs are thoroughly tumbled around. The next day you start up the next bottle, and so forth. Within 36 hours the little shrimp hatch. Now pour the contents of the bottle through the artemia strainer into a container. Thus you separate the egg shells from the shrimp. Throw away the water and shells and feed the shrimp to the fish immediately.

Watching and Wondering The World in the Water Droplet

Perhaps one day you weren't quite so precise about feeding as usual. Then the next day something like this could have happened to you: You turn on the light in the aquarium in the morning and everything seems normal at first. But after an hour you discover that there is a small, milky, dark cloud under the cover. If you were to look at it under the microscope, you would see many different tiny little animals, all trying to get to the light. They are parameciums, rotifers, and flagellates. You can find the little animals in any water drop, even if the water appears clear as glass. Only then the animals aren't so numerous.

How to Make a Tin-Can Magnifying Glass

You can make your own magnifying glass to better observe young fish and other small animals in your aquarium. To do this, take a large, empty can and have your parents remove the bottom of it. (There should be no rough edges, top or bottom.) Now you have a tube. At one end, stretch a piece of plastic wrap taut over the edges and fasten it with a rubber band. The magnifying glass is ready. When you hold the end with the plastic over it down in the water and look through the other end, you see everything in the aquarium enlarged (see drawing, page 59).

Impressive: The head of the Bristle Mouth Catfish.

The colorful White Cloud Mountain Minnows have a clearly visible neon stripe.

Snails in the Aquarium

Besides the fish and the tiny parameciums you can also find other animals in your aquarium, such as snails. Perhaps one day you discover a slimy deposit on the glass wall or on a leaf, and you can't easily scratch it off with your fingernail. Then you have most certainly found snail eggs, from which the young snails will develop. You can easily watch that take place right in front of you.

How to do it: Cut off the leaf with the eggs on it and put it in the guppy tank (see page 52). After some time you can see little red dots, which keep getting larger. They are usually red ramshorn snails. If you give them a food tablet every 5 days, they will grow quickly. Then you can transfer them to your large aquarium. You just have to watch out that you don't get too many snails in the aquarium (see page 48).

Useful Terms

T his list of Useful Terms explains the important terms used around the aquarium. Among them are also some technical words that appear on boxes of food or medication.

Artemia
Brine shrimp; they are good as food for raising fish fry.

Assimilation
In their green parts, the plants manu-facture the substances they need for growth, using water and carbon dioxide.

Bacteria
Single-celled small organisms, which are in the aquarium filter, in the ground material, and in the water; they break down waste products of the fish, rot-ting food, and plant remains.

Brine shrimp
see Artemia

Brood care
The parental behavior fish exhibit toward their young. The parents lead their fry to food and protect them from enemies.

Bubble nest
Labyrinth or Thread Fish build such nests on the water's surface and lay their eggs in it.

Daughter plant
Offshoots, in which first the leaves and then the roots develop.

Ectoparasites
Disease organisms, usually fungi and parasites, which locate on the mucous membranes of fish.

Encapsulate
To enclose against external influences.

Endoparasites
Disease organisms, usually worms and parasites, which locate in the skin or in the body of the fish.

Fungi
Plural of fungus; plants that lack chlorophyll and often cause disease in animals and plants.

Gonopodium
Male sex organ in the Live-Bearing Toothed Carps.

Guppy tank
Container for breeding in which the female lays eggs and the young sink through a grid to the bottom. They are thus separated from the mother, who would otherwise eat them.

Humic acid
see Tannic acid

Ich
Abbreviation for *Ichthyophtirius*; the name of the organism that causes white spot disease.

Labyrinth
An additional breathing organ in the Labyrinth Fishes, with which they can remove oxygen from the air.

Lateral line
A kind of radar on both sides of the fish's body from head to base of the tail. The lateral line allows the fish to estimate its distances from objects and other fish. Thus it is possible for fish to swim in a school without bumping into one another.

Leaf axil
The point at which the leaf grows from the stem.

Mother plant
Large, sturdy plant with offshoots.

Offshoots
Young plants that grow out from the mother plant.

pH value
Acid concentration of the water; it indicates whether the water is acidic or basic. The pH value can be mea-sured with a test kit (from the pet store).

Photosynthesis
Plants carry on photosynthesis by day. Using the energy of light, they turn carbon dioxide and water into sub-stances that they need to grow. In the process, oxygen is set free, a "waste product," as it were.

Pregnancy spot
See Spawn spot

With a homemade tin-can magnifying glass you can observe the aquarium's inhabitants even more clearly.

Pregnant
Carrying eggs in the body.

Rearing tank
Separate aquarium in which fish are placed to spawn. The fry can also be raised there until they are no longer likely to be eaten by the adult fish. Sometimes called a nursery tank.

Rhizome
Root form, from which a complete plant can develop from each leaf axil. First comes the leaf, then the root.

School
Many fish swimming together form a school, for instance Characins or Barbs. In the school they find protection from predators.

Slow-release fertilizer
Fertilizer that is usually surrounded by a layer of gelatin and thus releases its nutrients over an extended period of time.

Slow-release food
Food that is made available over an extended period of time; good to use if you are away from home for a few days.

Spawn
Fish eggs (noun); to lay eggs (verb).

Spawn spot
Pregnancy spot; dark egg spot on the rear body of female Live-Bearing Toothed Carps. The fertilized eggs with the young in them are visible through the skin of the fish.

Swim bladder
An organ that allows the fish to float underwater and move up or down without moving its fins.

Tannic acid
It makes water acid and turns it slightly yellow.

Thermometer
Temperature-measuring instrument with which the water temperature in the aquarium should be checked regularly.

Thermostat
Temperature regulator with which a certain temperature can be established in the heater.

UL
Abbreviation for Underwriters Laboratoroy. On electrical equipment, this abbreviation indicates that it has been checked for safety by experts.

Volt
Measure of electrical output.

Watt
Measure of current used by a piece of electrical equipment.

Index

Addresses and Literature

Associations

Breeder's Registry
(Journal of
  Maquaculture)
P.O. Box 255373
Sacramento, CA 95865
breeders@kplace.
  monrou.com

International Center for
  Living Aquatic Resource
  Management
MCPO Box 2631
0718 Makati M.M.
Philippines
j.mcmanus@cgnet.com

Marine Aquarium
  Societies of North
  America
(MACNA Conference)
P.O. Box 508
Penns Park, PA 18943

Periodicals

Aquarium Frontiers
P.O. Box 6050
Mission Viejo, CA 92690

Aquarium Fish Magazine
P.O. Box 6050
Mission Viejo, CA 92690

Journal of Maquaculture
Breeders Registry
P.O. Box 255373
Sacramento, CA 95865
tel. 1-916-487-3752

Makai
University of Hawaii Sea
  Grant College Program
1000 Pope Road
Room 200
Honolulu, HI 96822
tel. 1-808-956-8191

Marine Aquarist
Aquacraft, Inc.
P.O. Box 653
San Carlos, CA 94070
tel. 1-415-637-0322

Marine Fish Monthly
Publishing Concepts
  Corp.
3243 Highway 61
East Luttrell, TN 37779
tel. 1-423-992-3892

*Sea Grant in the
  Caribbean*
Sea Grant College
  Program
P.O. Box 5000 UPR-RUM
Mayaguez, PR 00681
tel. 1-809-834-4726

SeaScope
Aquarium Systems, Inc.
8141 Tyler Blvd.
Mentor, OH 44060
tel. 1-800-822-1100

The Armored Catfish pair has found a wonderful cave for a hiding place.

The Author
Peter Stadelmann has been a pet author for many years. He is a pet store dealer as well as a trainer and examiner of pet store salespeople for the Chamber of Trade and Industry in Nuremberg, Germany. For many years keeping aquariums has been an especially favorite hobby.

The Photographers
Hartl: pp. 12, 25 (bottom right); Kahl: pp. C2/1, 13, 21, 24/25 (top), 33, 37, 40 (top right; center left; bottom left; bottom center; bottom right) 53, 57; Kasselmann: p. 40 (top left); Linke: pp. 4, 5, 17, 20, 24 (center left), 25 (top right; center right; bottom left), 29 (bottom), 36, 48, C4; Nieuwenhuizen: pp. 16, 24 (top left), 29 (top; center), 44, 45, 56, 64/ C3; Reinhard: p. 24 (bottom left; bottom right); Sommer: p. 49; Spreinat: p. 32; Steimer: pp. C1, 9.

The Artist
Peter Fischer studied graphic design in Wuppertal, Germany, and has worked since 1976 as a free-lance illustrator for newspapers, book publishers, and advertising agencies. One focus of his work is the illustration of cookbooks and animal books.

The Photographs on the Covers
Front cover: The boy is about to catch a pregnant female Guppy with a fish net.

Back cover: A Ram pair guards its eggs.

English translation © Copyright 1998 by Barron's Educational Series, Inc.

© 1997 by Grafe und Unzer Verlag GmbH, München

Published originally under the title *Erlebnis Aquarium*

Translated from the German by Elizabeth D. Crawford.

Library of Congress Catalog Card No. 97-36748

International Standard Book Number 0-7641-0300-8

Library of Congress Cataloging-in-Publication Data
Stadelmann, Peter.
   [Erlebnis Aquarium.   English]
   Adventure Aquarium / Peter Stadelmann.
      p.   cm.
   Includes bibliographical references and index.
   ISBN 0-7641-0300-8
   1. Aquariums. 2. Aquarium fishes. I. Title.
SF457.S58513   1998
639.34—dc21   97-36748
                              CIP

Printed in Hong Kong
9 8 7 6 5 4 3 2 1

The Armored Catfish are the "health police" in a community aquarium. With their barbels they search the bottom, stones, roots, and plants for remains of food and other edible things. They help prevent the rotting of leftover food and maintain the water quality.